ORGANIZATION DEVELOPMENT

ORGANIZATION DEVELOPMENT

IDEAS AND ISSUES

Robert T. Golembiewski

Transaction Publishers
New Brunswick (U.S.A.) and Oxford (U.K.)

Copyright © 1989 by Transaction Publishers
New Brunswick, New Jersey 08903

All rights reserved under International and Pan-American Copyright Conventions. No part of this book may be reproduced or transmitted in any form or by any means, electronic or mechanical, including photocopy, recording, or any information storage and retrieval system, without prior permission in writing from the publisher. All inquiries should be addressed to Transaction Publishers, Rutgers—The State University, New Brunswick, New Jersey 08903.

Library of Congress Catalog Number: 88-15953
ISBN: 0-88738-245-2
Printed in the United States of America

Library of Congress Cataloging-in-Publication Data

Golembiewski, Robert T.
    Ideas and issues in organization development / Robert T. Golembiewski.
      p. cm.
    Includes index.
    ISBN 0-88738-245-2
    1. Organizational change. I. Title.
HD58.8.G643 1988   88-15953
658.4'06—dc19   CIP

Contents

Introduction

Organization Development: Ideas and Issues intends to mark the coming-of-age of a burgeoning area of practice, research, and theory. Now, this may seem a debatable basis for the present volume, but convenient chapter and verse support the conclusion opening this introduction.

Perhaps a decade ago, most of the literature looked at Organization Development (OD) with concerned and cautious eyes. Even OD supporters saw it in a delicate condition: it was in its adolescent phase, said some; others voiced significant doubts that OD supporters had retained that early fire in their bellies; and pessimism about success rates dominated, especially concerning applications in the public sector.

OD's opponents provided an even more somber picture, which does not surprise. We need not go into details, but one example suggests the sense of the broader pessimistic literature. OD was aptly named, went one canard—OD meant "overdosed," and that is what happened to many organizations exposed to Organization Development.

Today, the development challenges facing OD still remain great, not only are they under firmer management, but solid reasons for optimism also have surfaced. Consider only two points, which reinforce one another. After many false starts, ODers are well on their way toward testing a comprehensive statement of ethics and standards, which surely constitutes a significant sign of the area's coming-of-age. Earlier, neither the available wit nor will sufficed to surface such a document and to begin testing it with various interested publics. As a related sign of the status of OD, several recent waves of evaluative studies should hearten all but the most optimistic zealots. Success rates are substantial, we learn, and even formidable. To be sure, the existing literature has definite inelegancies. For example, some have criticized available studies in general for the lack of some of the technology of the natural sciences: control groups, random assignment of subjects, and other devices to reduce the probability that observed effects are due to factors other than specific OD designs. However, it remains far from clear that all such elements are either possible or desirable in OD research and applications. Moreover, such elements imply the need for fine tuning rather than basic rejection of existing OD research.

These signs of an emerging maturity in OD need not be taken on faith, and they should not, without qualification, be swallowed whole. For example, some of the criticisms of studies of OD applications make as much sense when applied to "action research" as they do to "straight science."

To illustrate, greater reliance on control or comparison groups in studies of OD applications would be helpful in establishing that any effects reported are due to OD interventions rather than to other factors—the passage of time, broad trends not due to the intervention, and so on. However, other criticisms of OD studies plainly do not make sense—like random assignment of subjects in team-building designs, for example. In addition, the strength of the effects reported in studies of OD applications do *not* seem to vary with the methodological rigor of individual studies.

Both the statement of ethics and standards as well as the success rates will have substantial later attention. So we need only note them here, since we can rely on what follows for many details and nuances.

This basic motivation of *Ideas and Issues* leaves open several questions, two of which will get direct attention. These two open questions are:

- Why the "ideas and issues" format?
- Who are the intended audiences of this book?

This book has a straightforward format, to begin with, and for quite direct reasons. Personal views, at times supported by empirical evidence, are expressed on a number of ideas and issues at the heart of OD. This reflects both an optimism and an intention, which are usefully described—following Dwight Waldo—in terms of "a solid core" and an "active periphery" that can be said to typify healthy areas of inquiry or application. Specifically, because OD rests on a substantial "solid core" of values and empirical regularities, one can meaningfully focus on a limited number of ideas and issues. Moreover, the existence of that central core creates not only a base from which extensions and extrapolations can be attempted but also induces a spirit which encourages such testing because it reduces defensiveness by aficionados.

This book implies not only a confidence that the OD core "*can take it*," in short, but also a conviction that the core "*must take it*" for purposes of both testing and future growth.

Hence, this book highlights the symbolic relationship between a "solid core" and an "active periphery." Without the former, OD would more likely stultify into an orthodoxy that both curbs enthusiasm and constricts development.

Hence, also this book's choice of an "ideas and issues" format, with a substantial list of topics on which the author outlines ideas, values, and feelings. These individual pieces might be called "essays," but that strikes me as too formal for what is intended here. Hence, let them be called "thought pieces," following the tradition of the *Pensées* by Blaise Pascal. Those ideas and issues at once relate to the solid core, and help define as well as test the active periphery.

Beyond these elementals, the book has a simple structure. Each part first briefly introduces the several thought pieces appropriate to OD ideas and issues. Part I deals with what OD is, Part II with what OD might become, and Part III with how to go from what OD is to what it might become.

Two caveats should not need making, but—hey—why risk any misunderstanding?

Caveat I.   This book's purpose is far less to air one person's views than it is to inspire an active dialog among and between numerous others. Directly, the goal of this book is not solitary and reflective reading. Much more, this book seeks to stimulate animated discussions of points of view, or even debates, which can both release energies and enlarge understanding. So the format of this book proposes, in effect, a two-stage exchange:

- Here are several ideas and issues, and also how I see them. The individual statements are brief, intentionally so, but they hopefully sketch coherent positions.
- In any case, how do you react to the ideas and issues, and to the statements developed about them? Especially if you do not like my formulations, how would you modify them?

This book assumes only two things, and these are best brought out front and center, and early in the game. Now is a good time to consider these ideas and issues, because the central core of OD is still forming. Moreover, now is a reasonable time to consider these ideas and issues because the central core is solid enough to support vigorous attention without coming unglued.

Caveat II.   This book makes no claim to having captured all of the appropriate ideas and issues, or even most of the significant ones. The book has corralled enough of the vital ideas and issues, I propose, to make the effort worthwhile. So readers may well wish to add numerous other possibilities and may even feel the urge to scrub some entries from the present list. So be it. Perhaps subsequent editions can profit from such industry, which is quite in keeping with the spirit of this volume.

But a second question remains open—what of the intended audiences for this book? That general question suggests a range of queries, in turn, two of which get specific attention here. Are these audiences tolerably targetable? And are there enough users out there to justify the expenditure of scarce capital and newsprint for the present set of ideas and issues?

Opinions may differ, but it appears to me that appropriate audiences in sufficient numbers exist. In part, my enthusiasm derives from the positive reception accorded to several of the selections below, which appeared in the "Process Observer" column in the *Organization Development Journal* (*O. D. Journal*). Through December 1987, in fact, sixteen of the thirty-four present selections have appeared there. Other pieces will be published in *O. D. Journal* while this book wends its way toward publication. All previously published selections have been edited, and often expanded, for present purposes.

But let us give explicit attention to likely users of this book, the readers of the *O. D. Journal* aside. Specifically, let me sketch four major interested parties to whom this book is targeted.

- Sales of OD texts and readers have been substantial over the last five to ten years, in both business and public management. This volume could well serve as supplementary reading for much of this course-taking public. Generally, the text or book of readings would supply the raw material for dealing with the present ideas and issues, as well as for testing the present format and its several variants.

  Would undergraduate as well as graduate course takers be reasonable users? Certainly. The latter subgroup might well utilize this volume, and many undergraduate courses also seem structured to employ this book to advantage.
- A very large number of people take workshops or short courses in OD, either for the first time, for consolidating past learnings, or being inspired to seek working answers to new questions or approaches to novel perspectives. The size of the potential audience defies even ballpark estimates, but it is large and growing and comes from all points of the functional and policy-arena compass: business, government, health care, education, the helping professions, and so on.

This volume should have a substantial relevance for this set of extramural or in-service audiences. The ideas and issues are often relevant for those seeking a clearer context for what they do, and how, and why. And the short essays provide useful foils for testing personal experiences and learnings, which can do double duty. Newcomers may be alerted by this book to dilemmas and challenges, and can experiment with how to deal with them, if only in a vicarious sense. More experienced folks may be motivated by this book to test and even transcend their hard-won views, in the process of subjecting the essays below to the heat and intensity of their experiences.

- I sense a new vitality among various professional groups which ODers call home—local units of the American Society for Training and Development, of the OD Network, of the Organization Development Institute, and so on. In addition to rest and recharging of the batteries—both vital activities—I sense a growing attention in such numerous membership groups to more narrowly professional concerns like those raised by the present set of issues and ideas.

The success of Peter Block's *Flawless Consulting* as a guide for discussion in such local meetings seems to me a harbinger of what we will likely see more, in a growing variety of forms for large numbers of users.

- Finally, OD seems to be "going international," in new and more determined ways than ever before. For example, I have seen firsthand the burgeoning of OD in western Canada over the past five or six years, and have even steered that development a bit. To a similar end, the Organization Development Institute and other OD associations have aggressively developed a worldwide presence in several ways. Moreover, for about two decades, OD has had an increasingly prominent role in various efforts to build institutions and capacities overseas—in rural and community development, for example, as well as in the managerial and high-tech applications often associated with "North American" or "Anglo" OD.

These international audiences are still a somewhat unknown quantity. But they would provide cross-cultural perspectives on this volume; and this book in turn might variously pose for them in useful ways those developmental challenges seen in their clearest form in North American OD.

Robert T. Golembiewski
March 1, 1988
Athens, Georgia

Part I

WHAT OD IS,
AND ASPIRES TO

Introduction

OD is protean and in-process, which defies a complete picture of "what OD is," but a baker's dozen of thought pieces do their best with a challenging assignment. The reader might usefully approach this first set of selections in terms of three organizing conventions:

- Selections 1 through 5 have a strong prescriptive character and emphasize what OD *should be*.
- Selections 6 through 10 focus on the description of what OD *is*—as a mixed rather than an ideal case, as a product of particular historic and developmental forces that give color and texture to OD.
- Selections 11 through 13 provide perspective on three specific challenges to OD in practice, and those three illustrate a much longer list of challenges.

1. What OD should be: selections 1 through 5.   Four thought pieces suffice to provide perspective on OD. Why so few? Well, readers of this book will not be neophytes. And why so many? Those readers nonetheless may need some sense of the author's map of the OD territory, at least as a take-off point for discussion if not debate.

Hence the five initial selections run the risk of being too much in one sense, and too little in another. But so be it. The selections are short, in any case, and will be amply backstopped by selections to come.

"A Rose by Any Other Name . . ." gets us going. The issue of what to call "it" at first did not much excite me, but there came a point in time when it became clearer that lines had to be drawn somewhere. In part, this growing realization derives from an escalating impatience about explaining away what other people call "OD" but which is not—or so it seems to me. In larger part, there are growing bodies of theory and experience that end up in pretty much the same place and develop quite similar approaches, even though the points from which they started were poles apart. Both theoretically and practically, these commonalities will profit from a common label, which will not only get people usefully connected and talking but also will reduce the need to reinvent the wheel if those people continue to act independently.

3

So both inclusion as well as exclusion motivate the first selection. Consider only the work in organizations which most observers label OD, and that effort in "developmental administration" variously called "institution-building," "capacity building," "community development," and so on. Only recently have the commonalities sufficiently surfaced to encourage what could have been usefully happening all along—cooperation and collaboration in doing what massively and obviously requires doing.

The first thought piece focuses on the usefulness of making both in and out distinctions, and the three following selections help explain why. Those selections in common provide some specifics about what constitutes "OD," given that it has been called other things.

"Process Observation as *the* Key" relates to a central commonality in OD, as the title notes. Focusing on what happens between people provides very useful input for efficient and effective living as well as working. The essential point can be expressed in numerous ways: e.g., it takes two (or more) people to really see one person. That conveys a lesson at the heart of human life. We learn from others: all individuals have a great capacity to delude themselves about themselves; and we can become in significant senses what others perceive (or misperceive) us as being or wanting. So we can all smile when we hear the story about the two psychiatrists. You know, one psychiatrist says to the other:

You're OK. How am I?

We smile, but we also understand.

OD seeks to do something *with* process analysis, in short, so as to do something *about* interpersonal and intergroup relations in organizations. The singular association of process analysis with OD constitutes a very powerful motivator for separating the proverbial sheep from the goats, when it comes to considering those who claim to do "organization development."

So great is the power of process analysis, however, that some people fall into the trap of concluding that all OD is interaction-centered, or that (not quite so expansively) all OD must begin with interaction-centered designs. "OD as Stool: Ruminations about a Metaphor" directs attention to this trap, and warns against it.

A focus on interaction is understandable, if it can be overdone. The focus on OD as interaction-only or as interaction-initially gets support from the power of directing attention to process issues, but owes most of its currency to the fact that in the earliest days the only *basic* OD learning approaches were interaction-centered. ODers initially were much impressed with the T-Group or sensitivity training, and later with its several modifications that became "team building." Only slowly were various structural and policy interventions—job enrichment, flexible work hours, and so on—added to the inventory of most ODers.

Part of the fascination with interaction also derives from the lack of explicit emphasis on the prescriptive aspects of OD. For example, the early OD literature abounds with circumlocutions—of designs that are "helpful" and of resources persons who "facilitate." The "why" of this helping and facilitating tended to get inadequate attention, and perhaps especially because the technology often seemed "to work."

"Why OD?: Putting Values in Their Prominent Place" seeks to rectify this imbalance, and to put the brakes on any technocratic tendencies. At base, OD is a profoundly moral enterprise, dealing as it ineffably does with the kind and character of relationships that should exist between people in collective settings. "Why OD?" makes that crucial point, early and up-front.

The focus on OD as value-loaded induces subtle but significant shifts in both thought and practice. For example, *the* issue ceases to be: Interaction-centered intervention or not? Rather, the focus shifts to meeting OD's values, whatever the character of the design or the mode of intervention. Many variants—of interaction, structure, and policy—can be put into the service of OD values; but those variants also can be put in the service of other values, even opposed ones.[1] So values have to occupy center stage, constantly.

Convenient lists of OD values exist in many sources,[2] but "OD as Increasing Responsible Freedom in Organizations" provides both convenient context for, as well as illustrations of, OD as value-loaded. The selection's emphasis is on a personally comfortable shorthand guide for what OD aspires to, with examples drawn from a contemporary public agency and also from the street people of Bombay, India.

2. OD as a mixed case: selections 6 through 10.   One's aspirations always are tethered—by time, circumstance, and fortune, whether good or bad. Five selections illustrate the point for OD. Basically, the ideal model becomes a mixed case under the impact of forces and personalities that seek their place in the conceptual sun.

Any active area of inquiry is an arena for contending formulations, to begin this introduction to a few of the factors seeking to pull OD this way, and to push it that way. This is far more a good thing than an awkward one, although the dynamics can be uncomfortable from time to time. Robust areas will not only survive such tests, but they must stimulate them and also thrive on them. Anemic areas should be devalued, or disappear entirely.

"OT and OD: Transformation, Fine Tuning, or Rechristening?" deals with one such case of helpful challenge. OT stands for Organizational Transformation, and constitutes either a perspective on OD, or an alternative to it. The thought piece below opts for the former view, but that is not particularly important. Identifying the challenge, and sketching the rationale for dealing with that challenge—these constitute the heart of the matter.

Next, a pair of thought pieces devote attention to "Some Differences Between OD Generations." It comes as no general surprise that a people-helping technology-cum-values should be influenced by the characteristics of the people who contribute to its development. The specifics of expressing this general point may contain kernels of useful informations and even insight, however.

The first of the pair dealing with personal impact focuses on "Four Generations and a Few Differentiae." In sum, OD reflects the contributions of at least four generations of scholars/practitioners, and multiple differences between them add flavor and nuance to the developing OD. The selection isolates several rosters of OD players: the few founding fathers; their selected recruits; an expanding network; and the subsequent contemporary cadres of ODers. In various ways, these four basic rosters are generally associated with differing experiences and priorities that have stamped OD, for good or ill, and ideally will amply inform OD even as those generations also induce tensions that could tear asunder OD's core.

The second of the pair of selections about OD generations deals with two critical differences between the four generations—"Socialization and Lode Stars." Briefly, the generations differ in how they were inducted into the legions of OD specialists in planned change, and these experiences constitute different lode stars, by which they guide their professional development and that of OD. For example, differences in elitist versus populist orientations are traced to different tendencies in socialization patterns, and these orientations remain to influence what people do, and why, in their professional practice and research.

The purpose in this pair of thought pieces is broadly descriptive, not pejorative. A healthy area of research and practice will not generate generations of clones, but will recognize generational differences and seek to extract energy from them. The two thought pieces seek to act on these two generalizations as well as to reinforce them.

The two selections on generational differences also serve to provide context for several other thought pieces, as is directly the case with "Two Faces of OD: Populism and Elitism." The tension seems to me a central one in OD and, like many tensions in the arena, it may profit from greater recognition and continuous constructive engagement, but it is unlikely to be resolved. But not to worry. That tension can be more a source of useful energy than a "problem," if correctly viewed. "Two Face of OD" seeks to provide this appropriate recognition, as well as to generate a modicum of the moderating influence that understanding can help bring.

Too much of even the best things are possible, of course, as we are reminded by "OD's Near-Term Destiny: Professional Maturation or Time's Dumpster?" The several fragmenting challenges to OD sketched here—and more could easily be added—promise no rose garden, but the game is still in the early innings. Specifically, "OD's Near-Term Destiny" sketches four priority elements in determining whether maturation *or* the dumpster will be the fate of the OD in the near future.

3. Specific challenges to OD: selections 11 through 13. The five selections just introduced suggest ODers will need nimble minds to constructively manage major historic and developmental forces. But where is this nimbleness particularly important? Let us be specific, via at least a few illustrations. Although the OD's life-chances also will be substantially influenced by how a whole class of specific challenges gets responded to, only three representatives of that class get attention in selections 11 through 13.

A first challenge relates to the ability of ODers to deal with immediate interests. These can be economic—as in the case of the thought piece entitled "The Yellow Envelope on the Floor." But the point applies broadly to other forms of self-interest—desires for status, professional recognition, acceptance or affection, and so on. "To deal with" in this case has no narrow meaning. It refers to satisfactory management of a problem area, as viewed internally. But it also refers to the public perception that OD's management of self-interest is in good shape, on average, given the nagging nature of the issues.

The first thought piece about self-interest is drawn from personal experiences, and may be too-colorfully entitled "The Yellow Envelope on the Floor: Does Paying the Piper Imply Calling the Tune?" It deals with drawing a fine line: How to respond to the needs of powerful clients, and yet respect the specialist's required autonomy and credibility. The focus is deliberately narrow, but the implications are as wide as all professional practice.

The usefulness of OD also will be influenced in significant measure by its reach-and-grasp when it comes to arenas of application. Some propose that OD is largely restricted to business settings, resting as it does on an industrial model of organizations. Others expand the fields of applications to problem situations encountered in public agencies, and far beyond.

Certainly, OD's usefulness will be affected by how this issue is worked out. A thought piece directs attention to the general question, and provides an orientation to a working answer. "Is OD Universalistic or Particularistic?: Some Similarities between Business and Public-Sector Consultation" advertises both the focus and the selection's basic position.

OD challenges also include the focus of a final selection in Part I—"Is OD Narrowly Culture-Bound?: Well, Yes; and Then, No." Patently, if OD is culture-bound that will restrict its applicability, perhaps severely.

The subtitle may seem to leave the issue hanging in the air. But the reader will have to wait on a reading of selection 13 to judge that issue, even in part. Indeed, the careful reader might reserve judgment for a longer time—if not until completing the volume, at least through the first three selections of Part II.

Notes

1. For a dramatic case, see Ethan A. Singer and Leland M. Wooton, "The Triumph and Failure of Albert Speer's Administrative Genius," *Journal of Applied Behavioral Science* 12 (Jan. 1976): 79–103.
2. For an overview, see Robert T. Golembiewski, *Approaches to Planned Change* (New York: Marcel Dekker, 1979), vol. 1, chaps. 1 and 2.

1

"A Rose by Any Other Name . . .": OD? OE? OI? HRD?

The issue of what to call "it" has been a hot one in recent years. Within the month, a publisher asked rhetorically whether I really wanted to use the term "organization development" in a book he was copyediting. He asked: "Will it be called OD in five years?" And several well-known consultants have publicly advised getting on with "it," by all means. But by no means should the label be "OD," they propose. Indeed, I heard one of those savants recently argue that the term OD had to go because of the awkward vernacular. That is, to some hearing the term, "OD" means to ingest too much of a harmful thing, and "overdosed" also may be associated with DOA, or "dead on arrival." Both are unattractive states, of course.

Whatever the reasons, no one can miss the many signs of acronymic agility concerning a common set of activities. A subsequent essay deals in some detail with one example of this offering of replacement designations—"OT and OD: Transformation, Fine Tuning, or Rechristening?" We had the U.S. Army's OE, or Organization Effectiveness, in addition, which was mostly survey/feedback but utilizes other well-known designs. And one of our major auto manufacturers has OI, which is Organization Improvement. OI relies mostly on creating high cohesive groups to induce and sustain behavioral change. This is, of course, team building with a work-methods orientation that is often called QC (or Quality Circles), except by our auto manufacturer. And others have argued that we need a very broad umbrella, like HRD (for Human Resource Development) to encompass "it."

Interpreting this industry presents some real problems. My earliest reaction to such rechristenings was laconic. "A rose by any other name . . . ," in short. As long as OD values get acted on—openness, owning, trust, and so on—why should it matter what designation or acronym people use? So I was an "easy rider" on the issue.

But more recently my view has changed.

What accounts for my change of mind, which is associated with a change in feeling? I am in touch with several contributors to change, which I offer here not only as personal perspectives but also as stimulants to the reader's decision making about creative rechristening.

The creative alphabetizations might simply be cases of NIH (or Not Invented Here), whose symptoms some thought alleviable by a rechristening. So the flurry of acronyms implies a statement of ownership by way of christening, which is an indirect way of saying that "it" has value and deserves special identification. This may seem innocent enough, or even laudatory, at first glance. But it does not represent the kind of thinking that (dare I use the term?) an OD consultant likes to see in a client. So why tolerate it among ODers, or OIers, or whatever?

Moreover, enthusiasm for renaming might reflect a kind of sectarianism or fractionating that has been enervating in other areas, and could also threaten OD's core values. Better to confront whatever issues underlie the impulses to differentiation, as opposed to tacitly buying into them or at least encouraging them by lack of concern about what "it" is called.

In addition, relabeling contributes to an ahistoricism, a neglect of the roots of development and the identification which they help foster. That sense is a costly one to give up, or even to threaten. Being one of a long line has useful motivating and disciplinary features, although on occasion it can induce a reactionary spirit.

Finally, I note in academic circles a kind of polysyllabic imperialism. Not infrequently, the revisionists seemed most interested in moving into a burgeoning area, often from areas that were having trouble getting students. That competition via assimilation was fine, as far as it went. But all too often those revisionists did not have the values I associate with OD, and hence they potentially threatened the essence although their approach was through the acronym. That would not wash.

Besides, I had a fondness for "OD." God knows why, but it was there. Certainly, paternity was not the issue, for "it" has been named long before I attained the semblances of professional reason.

For such reasons, then, I am more than a little pleased that The Process Observer appears in a periodical called *O. D. Journal*. Like all well-intentioned process observers, I will be looking at the scene and seeking ways that you and I can learn from the dynamics around us, hopefully with minimal defensiveness all-around, but on occasion risking that as well when the stakes seem appropriate.

So where do these considerations take me? On one hand, both Organization Development and OD eventually might have to go the way of all flesh; and there might be specific reasons why we might choose to be vague in naming "it," such as a finicky client whose recalcitrance on nomenclature might usefully be postponed for later attention.

On the other hand, there seem to me ample reasons why we should not be precipitous in adopting a new designation, of which I note only three here. Thus what I and others call "OD values" are not so robust and with such legions of effective and well-placed supporters that they are certain to survive, whatever their locus. Far from it, no doubt. Would "OD values" survive if the reference group were HRD? That is a big and variegated umbrella, and "HRD values" represent interests different from OD as well as more muscle. And the record for purely local initiatives—the "OI values" of the world, or the "walking counselors" of Hawthorne memory—is somber. If its practitioners do not become "servants of power," they often are sorely tempted to do so. And the status given by local nomenclature can be withdrawn locally, as has recently occurred with OE in the U.S. Army.

In addition, there are hopeful stirrings that suggest a certain coming of age in OD, in matters big and small. Thus I am now reading *Organization Development in Transition: Evidence of An Evolving Profession.*[1] That has a nice ring to it, which the volume's substance supports, as far as my reading has gone. And the big-muscled American Society for Training and Development recently released its "competency study" of standards of performance in nine areas, including Organization Development.[2] To a similar point, see especially one later essay—"A Statement of Values and Ethics"—which refers to a long-delayed and very welcome step in OD's coming-of-age. These are hopeful signs, if hardly definitive, they may replace the malaise common in OD circles in recent years—questions of an unresolvable identity crisis, of awkward adolescence, of where to go next, and so on. We will have to wait and see, of course, but there seems no reason for shucking the OD label that has brought us to this point of possible take-off to a more impactful and less conflicted future.

Finally, and personally, your Process Observer retains a fondness for "OD." God knows why, but it is there. Hence the title of this book, and its effort to circumscribe a profession—thereby adding definition to OD, by extending the concept in some senses and crimping it a bit in other particulars.

Notes

1. A. J. McLean, D. B. Sims, I. L. Mangham, and D. Tuffield, *Organization Development in Transition: Evidence of an Evolving Profession* (New York: Wiley, 1982).
2. Patricia A. McLagan and David Bedrick, "Models for Excellence," *Training and Development Journal* 37 (June 1983): 10–20.

2

Process Observation as *the* Key: Where and When to Practice Skills

The core skills of OD intervenors certainly lie in "process observation"—the focus on what is going on between individuals and groups, for the purpose of helping people understand and cope with those dynamics. This develops a greater consciousness of the products of human interaction for the purpose of transcending those products—becoming more the master of our processes by an awareness of them, and adapting them to our purposes by greater consciousness of them. As distinct from the "expert model," Schein's central and early book defines "process consultation" as "a set of activities on the part of the consultant which helps the client to perceive, understand, and act upon process events which occur in the client's environment."[1]

Fate was kind in earlier days. T-Groups or sensitivity training were in full bloom in the 1960s, and their major attractions included the intensive opportunity for many to hone skills of process analysis and intervention. Facilitators at many levels of skill and experience saw their interventions unfold over extensive periods of group time; and trainers often would get honest and caring feedback about their efforts.

These opportunities were particularly rich where the National Training Laboratories (NTL) sponsored large and growing programs of laboratories for general clients and for different levels of managers. Such locations had a high density of trainers with whom notes could be shared, and co-training was common and valued by such NTL administrators as Lee Bradford. Talk about process interventions dominated, and skills as well as attitudes were on display for extended intervals in the presence of valued fellow professionals. This provided rich opportunities for getting sharp, and staying sharp, in process observation. Perhaps even more important, one's confidence level was tested, and one could calibrate and recalibrate one's intervening dials for later and lonelier situations—when to go ahead confidently, when to be cautious, and when to seek help.

University campuses also were a tumultuous cacophony of talk in T-Groups and various "support groups," affording splendid experience for numerous facilitators of all levels of competence. At one technical university in 1972, in fact, I counted over 100 courses and other experiences devoted to interpersonal process. Those days are long gone, although the availability of group experiences on campuses has not been reduced as much as most commentators assume.

The 1960s and early 1970s also were the salad days for practicing process observation in industry and government. In one corporation, for example, approximately 750 individuals attended voluntary one-week sensitivity-training experiences on company time, over several years in different formats for various purposes,[2] beginning with the most senior levels. The prime goal was to give participants a vivid sense of a different kind of interaction than they typically encountered at work. But major secondary goals related to developing a cadre of internal resources by serving as co-trainers with an external person in each T-Group. The co-trainers were all in personnel and HRD positions, and their valued T-Group assignments would sharpen useful process observation skills and techniques while expanding their range of comfortable intervention. Relationships of trust also would develop between participants and co-trainers, we hoped, and these could later be used back home to build greater openness into workday activities.

Since serendipity probably will not strike again in such ways, this thumbnail history of days past implies two central questions.

First, will ODers, and especially would-be ODers, get extensive practice with process observation, in situations of substantial duration and intensity having a high probability of honest and caring feedback?

This question encourages a typical response: Yes, but. NTL and others are still running T-Groups, but at sharply diminished levels. And programs emphasizing process-observation skills are fielded by NTL, University Associates, and several universities, but they are expensive and for small numbers. In addition, prodigious numbers of OD resources were turned out by some organizations, such as the U.S. Army, but they focus for understandable reasons on survey feedback. Moreover, although team-building is common, such efforts provide less generous and benign nurture for co-facilitation and for practice than did T-Groups. The time frames are tight; the stakes can be high; resources often are stretched too thin to justify co-facilitators; and opportunities for feedback from participants are diminished. Finally, various gatherings of the clan—at the periodic meetings of the OD Network, the OD Institute, and so on—have major value. But those precious occasions seem to me far more oriented to sharing "advanced techniques," or for just plain conviviality, than for basic attention to process observation.

Other essays in this series detail a variety of trends and pressures, moreover, that encourage a different way of expressing this "Yes, but" response to the first key question about practice with process observation. The modification that comes to mind may be too cute, but to me it does the job:

Yes, there will continue to be opportunities for gaining experience with process analysis, *but* the constraints on doing so not only are great, they also seem to be growing at an increasing rate. For details, consult numerous other pieces below, perhaps especially two detailing "Some Differences Between OD Generations," and single sections on the themes "Why OD?" and "Not Whether to Market, but What."

Second, does it make any difference whether fulsome opportunities for experience with process observation exist?

Here I have a bias, if not an answer. The lack of such opportunities will make a profound difference, as a single point should make clear. OD is, or should be, value-loaded. And process observation and intervention provide the best real-time experience with such values—not just lip service, but the honest-to-goodness testing of trust in the process of acting on those values, face to face, with minimal opportunity to hide behind specialized knowledge such as that relevant in much survey feedback, and with maximum exposure to the consequences of testing and trusting.

So I have a nagging concern that we may be living off our inheritance, distancing ourselves from the powerful dynamics and values that put the money in the bank in the first place. ODers have rightly raised the ante in an important regard: What OD intervenors should know about the scientific aspects of what they do, and why, have sharply increased, and for good reasons. This piece proposes that we devote more attention to how to at least stand still in the even more critical matter of fostering opportunities for growthful experience with process observation. Even better reasons support this second heightening of attention.

Notes

1. Edgar H. Schein, *Process Consultation: Its Role in Organization Development* (Reading, Mass.: Addison-Wesley, 1969), 9. See also Vol. 2, published in 1987.
2. Reports of some of this work found their way into the literature, typically with coauthors who were external and internal resources. See Robert T. Golembiewski and Stokes B. Carrigan, "Planned Change in Organization Style Based on Laboratory Approach," *Administrative Science Quarterly* 15 (March 1970): 79–93.

3

OD as Stool:
Ruminations about a Metaphor

Like all people, I rely on simple symbols as a convenient shorthand for more complex realities. For example, almost everyone recognizes that a sign featuring a knife and fork indicates a place to eat—a restaurant, or a snack bar. And if that sign has a diagonal red stripe superimposed over the knife and fork, most of us would know we will have to go hungry until we find an unstriped sign.

So it is for me with OD, which deals with a challenging and complex integration of values, empirical theories, and technologies for guiding praxis. I know something about this challenging complexity, but I often deal with it in radically simplified terms—like right now.

Specifically, I see OD as a stool, and have long done so. I realize that both designations and denotations of the word "stool" can differ. But I here refer to the furniture sense of stool, which can be depicted (very roughly) as:

And I suppose I will continue to think of OD as stool, perhaps especially because I did so for some time before anyone alerted me to other possible denotations/designations of "stools."

I admit, however, to being pleased by some of those other denotations/ designations, and especially one of them. Oh, you know the one I mean. To many African tribes, the stool (as furniture) was the symbol of authority, and the "golden stool" was of course associated with the highest authority—gold because, I suppose, Africans of that day had not been exposed to platinum or other more precious metals. Some Africans used the term, indeed, even when there was no literal stool. Representatives of colonial powers learned of this subtlety the hard way, on occasion having exerted prodigious efforts to find the "golden stools" they heard being talked about, but which they did not pause to understand more fully, in the heat of their covetousness.

OD to me is like both the literal and figurative sense of "stool," as I can establish in a brief but confidently suggestive way.

Literally, a three-legged stool suggests both effectiveness and efficiency. The metaphor suggests stability, without overdoing it. To paraphrase the Audi commercial of a few years back: Two legs are too few for stability, and four are too many. Literally, also, I identify each of the three legs with labels that relate to classes of interventions.

The sense of stool as OD symbol is direct. What might be called full-term or stable OD has three "legs"—*interaction* relates to the quite specific patterns of relationships that should exist between people and groups, as well as to the culture of beliefs and values that both guide and constrain those relationships; suitable *structure* is needed to provide form for the normative spirit of OD cultures; and appropriate *policies and procedures*, such as those associated with pay and recognition, also must reinforce both OD interaction and structure.

The sense of the imagery can be extended. Should the OD stool have only one or two legs, trouble might well be expected. The one-legged—or even two-legged—stools require a delicate balancing act, lest that stool topple over. This imbalance often occurred in OD practice, and not only in the early days when interaction approaches to OD—especially using the T-Group—dominated. Not infrequently, for example, OD participants might come to explicitly understand the patterns of interaction they desired, but be frustrated in acting on that understanding by existing but awkward structures or policies and procedures. For example, this was a common outcome when the bureaucratic model prescribed an organization's structure which, more or less, was usually the case. OD interaction implies high openness and high trust, that is to say, but the bureaucratic model is built on an assumption of the low trustworthiness of individuals which encourages low openness. This presents a scenario for dashed expectations and cruel frustration. Interaction approaches to OD were more hopeful than informed. The expressed hope was that, once an OD culture had been established, appropriate structures along with suitable policies as well as procedures would evolve, more or less as day follows night.

To extend this last notion, the night often proved a long one. Bureaucratic structures and policies/procedures proved very resilient and resistive, even when interaction-centered designs had done their work well. "Good work," in this connection, means that organization members developed a heightened sense of what relationships they preferred as people, and experienced a clearer sense of the gap between those preferences and what their organization's structures/policies implied, encouraged, or demanded. And such "good work'' dealing with interaction and relationships could have paradoxical effects, as in heightening frustration about work life or deepening despair that change was not possible. Typically, awkward structures and policies/procedures would inhibit movement toward the kind of interaction that even large majorities of organization numbers preferred. In part, this was due to lack of knowledge about specific structures and policies/procedures appropriate for OD. In larger part, probably, the problem lay not in anticipating the need for quick change in structures and policies/procedures, or in coming too late to that knowledge.

Indeed, often enough to be of very real concern, some evidence implies that appropriate interaction at least in cases should better—perhaps, could only—follow substantial changes in structures as well as in supporting policies and procedures. The usual front load in OD, in sum, could become the back load. Generally, this was particularly the case where the ''technical quotient'' was high and where work relationships were routinized and patterned—as at lower levels of organization, and especially so in manufacturing or assembly-line operations.

The issue is neither cut-and-dried nor cost-free. Whether and how to go with a front load of structure and or policies/procedures cannot be specified in detail, and tricky problems inhere in acknowledging on occasion the primacy of structure and policies/procedures. For example, an emphasis on structures and policies/procedures could threaten the involvement and ownership of participants, for most relevant expertise about structure/policies/procedures is in the hands of those comfortable with the expert or medical models: diagnosing for others, and prescribing for them. The interaction-centered approach increases the probability of both involvement and ownership by associating participants intimately with both diagnosis and prescription, in contrast.

So the visual sense of a three-legged stool serves me well. It summarizes the essential thrust of OD, reminds me of the basic requirements for designing a full-scale OD program, and it also tickles my conceptual funny-bone.

4

Why OD?
Putting Values in
Their Prominent Place

OD has dealt unevenly with its underlying values, which may not be news but still has an overarching significance. The associated problems cannot be resolved here, but even highlighting them will help.

Three models for dealing with values get brief attention—they include needs, instrumentalities, and right-on models. The biases of this editorial writer should be plain, at the start. That last appellation does not qualify as objective or neutral, or course. Hopefully, later analysis will demonstrate that the label is accurate.

The several "needs models" helped with value issues even as they neglected them. The Maslowian pyramid, McGregor's Theory X and Y, Herzberg's motivators versus satisfiers, and Argyris's dimensions for self-actualization, among numerous similar efforts, all illustrate needs models.

The several needs models seemed a pretty good deal, if one did not look too closely. They provided useful guidelines about *what to do*, in sum, but only fragile support for why. This made needs models vulnerable. They once dominated the behavioral science landscape, but have a sharply diminishing prominence these days.

Consider a few details. Needs models propose that "healthy" or "self-actualizing" individuals have internal gyroscopes which guide them, whenever the environment permits, and often even when that environment is overtly hostile. So there were only corrupt institutions which, once set aright, would allow individuals to be their inherently good selves.

So far, not so bad, as a first approximation. But needs models usually were presented as having only naturalist or empirical foundations; and this characteristic has increasingly done them in. Few OD ideologues said so directly,[1] although some others no doubt meant it: "We follow this or that needs model because it generally seems right and, given our present lights, morally preferable. And it's also nice that it tends to work, by and large, toward employee

satisfaction and productivity, 'it' being reflected in such forms as job enrichment, various participative forms, flexible work hours, regenerative interaction, and so on. These techniques do not always work, of course, but often
enough to make a practical difference.''

The naturalistically based strategy had a central weakness. Conquer by empirical fact, in effect, and you die the same way. The moral debate never got
started over whether we *ought to do* Theory Y, or the Argyrian dimensions, or
whatever. Attention got focused on the *is*, on what exists. And some
unanticipated is-es won a huge and growing victory over the several needs
models:

- You can't identify or measure the "needs" precisely, so we can't really
  know what proportion of the population in fact behaves which part of the
  time as if the gyroscope were operating.
- There are bad people—or enough people acting in awkward ways, enough
  of the time—to urge caution about which ways people will behave if their
  institutions unshackle them. "They" might simply trash the organization
  foolish enough to give them any leeway.
- Enough frustration exists in many people that "they" burn cities, knock
  over banks for obscure radical causes, and God knows what all.

Bennis put it appropriately. Something awkward happened on the way to
the naturalist, positivist, humanist future. Empirical data said so.

Such is-es would not destroy a value-based strategy, of course. They might
well strengthen that strategy, in fact, and encourage greater efforts to realize
the normative vision.

"Instrumentalities models" focus, in contrast, on *how to do*. A chilling
version of this approach, for example, sees OD as a "maturing industry."[2]
And maturing industries have several features: markets stabilize or shrink,
price competition escalates, claims about products grow increasingly
exuberant, ethical standards become increasing drags on marketing
flexibility, and so on. In another version, the emphasis is on mindless application of what we know how to do rather than on what should be done: packaged
nonverbals, canned designs for standard team building, T-grouping for the
world's population, and so on and on.

Instrumentalities models have a real place, but only for a limited and limiting question: How to do?

So the needs models have a fatal defect as a guide for OD; and instrumentalities models do not have even the real but flawed saving graces of the needs
models. Hence the priority for a strong dose of "right-on models," those that
deal directly with the big questions: *What should be done? OD for which
specific normative ends? Why OD?*

Providing a "why?" for OD gets powerful support from today's blockbuster in the management literature. Peters and Waterman emphasize that excellent firms are characterized by a deep sense of the need for meaning—a transcendence of the mundane via values and cultures in which people and organizations are embodied. They note that "he who has a *why* . . . can bear almost any *how*."[3]

Hence this editorial's title. OD has always been value-loaded, in fact. Witness the emphases on helping relationships and on learning communities, for example, as well as on such normative ways and means as openness, owing, and trust.[4] But OD has not always powerfully acknowledged these value bases of how it seeks to induce alternative cultures at work as well as in other areas of life. Hence also our need to do better in this critical regard.

My preferred way of indicating briefly the normative thrust of OD involves four variables—openness, owning, risk, and trust.[5] These variables have an operational quality, and overlay that are usually called OD's meta-values—a spirit of inquiry, intentional helpfulness in human relationships, a community of learners, and so on.[6] But let us focus on the operational level of four variables, which can be introduced briefly using this book as a context for description. When I write I am pleased with this book, although it differs greatly from most of the work I am associated with, I am being *open* and *owning*. Most of my other publications in the last decade or two emphasize empirical and statistical treatment, in sum, and no one has ever accused me of brevity. In addition, there is some *risk* in such a venture—an objective danger that what pleases me may be censured. But I have substantial *trust* that I and others can learn from this volume, however it is evaluated.

Conveniently, I think of these four variables as defining a significant-continuum—from regenerative to degenerative systems of interaction. One can visualize the two sets of extreme combinations of the four variables in this simplified way:

Degenerative		Regenerative
Low	openness	High
Low	owning	High
High	risk	Low
Low	trust	High

Table 4.1.   Two Idealized Systems of Interaction

Ample evidence suggests the two patterns of interaction are self-reinforcing and self-heightening. In regenerative interaction, as it were, one cannot lose for winning. In degenerative interaction, the persons-in-interaction do not get a break: they cannot win for losing.

It makes a very considerable difference which system tends to dominate interaction in a specific setting. In brief, degenerative interaction has this catalog of awkward consequences, among others:

- people will tend not to surface the real problems, ideas, or feelings;
- hence even hard work is not likely to result in solving problems that stay solved: oppositely, solving the wrong problem is likely to induce other and even less-tractable problems;
- consequently, in early encounters, people will feel a diminished sense of psychological success in degenerative systems;
- once a degenerative system exists, people will tend to variously withdraw from them—either physically or psychologically—and to disparage them;
- degenerative systems may be conflictful, as a result, but they more likely will be characterized by low levels of energy;
- norms will develop which reinforce withdrawal and low energy, and such forces patently are self-reinforcing; they discourage surfacing real problems, solving them, and so on.

In a few words, degenerative systems feed on themselves in self-limiting ways. Regenerative interaction is also self-reinforcing, but in more positive ways.

OD's challenge is evident in terms of these two systems. One goal is to create regenerative interaction, wherever possible. The second major goal is to inhibit or reverse degenerative interaction, wherever and whenever it exists.

There seems no need to understate OD's normative thrust, as expressed above. Almost all persons prefer regenerative interaction, even when they conclude it cannot be approached in some specific situation. And there seems plenty to do in the terms sketched above, even discounting those cases said to be unredemptively degenerative.

Notes

1. For one of those solitary and rare voices, see Robert Ross, "OD for Whom?" *Journal of Applied Behavioral Science* 7 (Sept. 1971): esp. 581–82. One could well argue that native cunning rather than mindless neglect was the determining factor, given the relativist and positivist tenor of the 1950s and 1960s. That was no period for "dogma," or even "moral precepts." I recall my own book—*Men, Management and Morality* (New York: McGraw-Hill, 1965). "Change the title,

you damn fool,'' a friend advised. ''Nobody who counts will admit reading it, even if they did.'' My friend was correct, I fear.

2. Terence C. Krell, ''The Marketing of Organization Development,'' *Journal of Applied Behavioral Science* 17 (July, 1981): 309–23.

3. Thomas J. Peters and Robert H. Waterman, Jr., *In Search of Excellence* (New York: Harper & Row, 1982), 76.

4. For details, see Robert T. Golembiewski, *Approaches to Planned Change* (New York: Marcel Dekker, 1979) 1, especially chaps 1 through 3.

5. *Approaches to Planned Change,* 58-69.

6. Ibid, 85-94.

5

OD as Increasing Responsible Freedom in Organizations

My mother, bless her soul, had a strong interest in what her son did as a consultant, but I do not believe our many talks really satisfied her in this regard. What I described, I remain convinced, she saw dimly, as behind a cloud of gentle disbelief, even doubt. Getting brought up-to-date had a ritual quality to it, for both of us. "So what did you do on your last consulting trip?," she might inquire. I would oblige in as general terms as I could get away with.

"And why would they want you to help in that?" she would probe.

"For the same reason that I like you to make pierogi," I would reply. "You're good at it."

Much the same seems true of most of those "in OD." They face similar requests to explain what they do, and why. For example, consider the broad range of definitions generated by a dozen or so specialists.[1] They were asked: What is OD? And their responses are a sight to see. Like a covey of quail, they at times share a common conceptual territory. Thus they almost unanimously emphasize the importance of process issues, and the significance of cultural change at work that can absorb substantial time and energies. Also like a covey of quail, once set a-flying from their smallish shared turf, the expert commentators definitionally whiz this way, and that. Just like a busted covey of quail, these experts are splendid to view, and often hard to follow.

For my purposes, I finally hit on an approach that is satisfying, at least to me. What do I do as an OD consultant, and why? *I try to help increase responsible freedom for those in organizations, and also for myself*, on balance.

Most people get the idea, without much elaboration of why. What Rousseau articulates with philosophical deftness, people know in their bones. Organizations imply role specialization, and that generates complex and often conflicting we/they pairs: management and labor, line and staff, headquarters and the field, and so on and on. This we/theyness reduces everyone's freedom, Rousseau proposes. Freedom exists to the degree that the "I" or "we" are in fact the "they." Otherwise, some authoritative "they" will exercise hegemony over a "we" or "I," and the latter's freedom consequently will be limited.

Since role specialization and limitations on freedom will always be with us in organizations, there will be plenty to do under the general heading of increasing responsible freedom.

The irony is that role specialization provides the vehicle for dealing with the consequences of role specialization, and so the palliative also implies a bit more of the disease. Management activities often limit freedom; and ODers specialize in reducing the probability of such limitations, or at least ameliorating their consequences. At the same time, however, ODers may be seen as—and may act in ways that actually result in—reducing the freedom of others. For example, ODers can at once help facilitate what a line official desires, but they can also serve to inhibit such desires. And that's the way it should be, in general, even though in specific cases ODers may ineptly restrict the freedom of all involved, including themselves.

I have in mind the aftermath of a successful team-building exercise, in one part of which a CEO contracted with his subordinates to extend insurance coverage to the partners of employees—whether the pairs are married or not, and without regard to the gender of such partners. The decision was not a casual one, and the issues had been massaged to a fault, if anything. The period was the mid-1970s, and the organization governmental. The CEO exacted a high price for his concession, in fact, with his subordinates agreeing in writing to several CEO preferences by way of a *quid pro quo*.

A bit later, the CEO thought better of the matter, and proceeded to make other arrangements with the insurer.

I had been the team-building facilitator, and came to have knowledge of what the CEO had done via a phantom note. The resulting dynamics can be sketched briefly. Although I did not know the identity of my informant, I had ample reason to believe the authenticity of the message. So I checked it out with the CEO, who first waffled and then admitted his reversal of what he had agreed to do in a group setting. "I'll take my chances when they find out about it," he noted as he speculated that might not be for three months or more. "And who knows? By then, my people might think differently about a position that really relates to just a few people, but is potentially bad press and goes against my moral grain in the bargain. A few zealots just roiled the waters, but people will see more clearly after a while."

I could not assent to the CEO's attempt to buy time, and (I assured him) major trouble as well. My view was direct, induced in about equal proportions by conscience and by my desire to preserve credibility in the eyes of others in the team-building exercise. I would not be a Pied Piper for hire, as it were, serving a CEO who would change consensual marching orders as he willed. Should he persist, I saw only two alternatives: he could reassemble the "team" to reconsider the full contracting; or he would force me to inform others how the CEO proposed to change the contract.

In brief, the CEO sought license while I (and others, I believed) had contracted for responsible freedom.

Now, it is not always easy to define "responsible freedom" in advance, as it applies to a specific case. I had no philosophical problems coming to a decision in the case just abstracted, given the acute practical difficulties of dealing with that CEO. Both the CEO and his first reports had traded away some things for others that they very much desired, after extended and open discussion, in a group setting that produced a written document describing who had agreed to do what, and for which *quid pro quo*.[2] Both parties were seeking greater freedom, in what I then perceived (and still do) as responsible ways.

The two alternatives I posed for the CEO reflected my sense of responsible freedom in the matter. Only license could legitimate other courses of action, I concluded then and believe now. I could not take refuge in "not knowing." I had not only been informed by an anonymous but clearly knowledgeable source, but confirmation came from the CEO himself, if grudgingly. Nor was there some convenient someone to whom I could "give the ball."

The more general case for "responsible freedom" has been discussed in detail elsewhere,[3] so it does not require repeating here even if the available space could contain the argument. But a tolerable working definition of "responsible freedom" generally features simultaneities, as when some intervention or agreement meets employee needs and at the same time has little or no cost to management or leads to conditions that management favors—e.g., heightened quality or productivity.

One point about "responsible freedom" does need underscoring, however. Traditionally, *the* approach to it has been through interaction-centered designs. People speaking openly and with trust would not only reduce repression, but also increase responsibility in response to feedback from those involved. Perhaps interaction-centered designs are even the *best way*. But an earlier essay—"OD as Stool"—explains why interaction-centered designs have no monopoly in OD, and that theme needs reinforcing here. Directly, interaction-centered designs are never sufficient. Moreover, they can even be dangerous.

As for the first qualifier on the efficacy of interaction-centered designs, OD is better seen as including designs that emphasize two other approaches: by way of structure, as well as by way of policies and procedures. That trio of approaches is required to reinforce one another in all full-scale, full-term OD applications. Otherwise, one can generate awkward (and all-too-common) outcomes—for example, interaction-centered designs can highlight the desirability of trust while a prevailing bureaucratic model for organizing rests on mistrust, and goes on generating it unless appropriate structural changes are made. Such forces in opposition not only will frustrate. A "successful" OD effort also may induce cynicism—expectations are raised and sensitivities become heightened, but nothing else changes.

And what of the reference to interaction-centered designs as dangerous? An extreme example occurred in Poland recently, where western ODers in general encouraged their Polish counterparts to "be open" with their officialdom as a prelude to constructive social renewal. Generally, Poles acknowledged, upward communication did have the character of much-varnished truth. On the whole, however, the Poles took this advice—altogether appropriate in other settings, and an ideal everywhere—as an invitation to "commit suicide." Only the extreme politeness of the Poles prevented an angry reaction to the sincere but obtuse insistence of the Westerners.

Of course, openness can be counterproductive or even poison in many other systems, or with specific individuals, at least at particular points in time. Consider the appropriate response when a boss asks his subordinate, in effect: "Tell me enough about yourself so that I can make a good case to fire you."

More generally, autocratic systems do not eagerly embrace open and honest communication. But progress toward responsible freedom in such systems— granted that such progress will be limited—can be made by way of appropriate changes in structure or in policies and procedures. These can serve OD values—in moderated ways, but nonetheless usefully, at least for openers.[4] After all, the OD goal involves moving systems from "where they are" toward OD ideals. That may be a very long trip in many cases, and one often better conceived as a set of incremental if nonetheless determined steps, rather than as a great leap forward.

Notes

1. See Donald Warrick, editor, "Definitions of OD by the Experts," *OD Newsletter*, Academy of Management (Winter 1978), 2–3.
2. The design closely followed Roger Harrison's "role negotiation" exercise. See his "Role Negotiation: A Tough-Minded Approach to Team Development," 84–96, in W. Warner Burke and Harvey A. Hornstein, eds., *The Social Technology of Organization Development* (Washington, D.C.: NTL Learning Resources Corp., 1972).
3. The point has been developed in several of my books, including: *Men, Management, and Morality* (New Brunswick, N.J.: Transaction, 1988); and *Approaches to Planned Change* (New York: Marcel Dekker, 1979), 2 vols.
4. For examples of serving OD values by means of changes in structure and in policies/procedures, see my *Approaches to Planned Change* (New York: Marcel Dekker, 1979), vol. 2.

6

OT and OD: Transformation, Fine Tuning, or Rechristening?

Organization Transformation constitutes a still small but rapidly growing prominence on the horizon of conscious change. Multiple signs testify to its emergence. Thus John Adams offers *Transforming Work*[1] as an early OT statement. And Richard Beckhard chose the occasion of an invited lecture as a distinguished change agent to speak on the theme: OT, fad, or imperative?[2] He came down, on definite balance, on the imperative side of the ledger.

What seems a reasonable positioning of OT, at least at this early time? Consider only this casually defined continuum: fine tuning through fundamental redefinition of major concepts and values associated with the label "OD."

The best available evidence does not imply that OT represents a transformation. The point can be made by reference to one of OT's leading figures, John Adams. Consider his circumscription of OT, which involves a comparison with OD. He writes:[3]

> Reflecting its academic roots, OD efforts have always been based on theories and the collection and analysis of data. I do not view OT as rejecting theory and data by any means, but it does somewhat shift the focus to establishing a vision of what is desired and working to create that vision from the perspective of a clearly articulated set of humanistic values. OD would not reject vision and values either—it's a matter of shifting the emphasis slightly towards a larger, more proactive perspective.

The longer version of points of difference with OD does not alter this picture in any fundamental way. In his catalog of particulars, to illustrate, Adams emphasizes six OT themes:[4]

- Vision, or the importance of purposes, goals, and directions
- New perspectives, or the questioning of assumptions made in organizations
- Energy field, or an emphasis on the managing of organization *processes* as well as *positions*

27

- Leadership, or the motive force required to realize the "new perspectives"
- Performance excellence which, in general terms, refers to the competent implementation of the vision
- Human empowerment, or the creation of environments in which human potentials can be achieved.

These themes orient more decisively toward fine tuning than transformation. That is to say, for example, it would help OD were its proponents to pay more explicit attention to the values underlying it. This point gets emphasis at several points in this collection of essays, in fact, and especially in "Why OD?" So Adams's attention to the point is most welcome, but it hardly constitutes a transforming view. In general, the themes fit quite comfortably (for example) into any OD text I know. Paramountly, in addition, the values underlying OD and Adams' OT seem very similar.

The point can be made by another go-around. Two OT themes—leadership and performance excellence—do get less-prominent attention in many OD sources. Thus facilitative activities get most attention in OD—or *got* such attention in early OD—while Adams proposes that OT will place more emphasis on architectural and perhaps advocacy activities. And OD often gives primary attention to "good processes," which at least in the long run will be more likely than "bad processes" to lead to "good performance."

Surely, however, even these two OT themes relate to fine tuning rather than transformation. They involve differences in degree rather than in essence.

Now, good general reasons support the equivalent of a vigorous periodic housecleaning—of figuratively sweeping out some cobwebs, applying the scrubbing brush, letting light in dark corners, and so on. So the OT thrusts have much to recommend them.

But this recommendation requires a basic qualification. Unless OT is positioned quite differently than seems to be the present case, I see no great likelihood that it will transform OD. This positioning of OT as basically fine tuning does not intend to demean or belittle, as noted. The present intent is to describe what seems to exist and, even more so, to encourage appropriate expectations. Fine tuning is not transformation, and any expectations to the contrary may be raised but probably only to be dashed.

Let me approach in another way the central conclusion that OT is unlikely to transform OD. We need to acknowledge that an incautious emphasis on OT, as presently circumscribed, may lead only to a kind of rechristening, and this possibility has a real down-side potential. What are the virtues of such rechristening? Well, among other effects, it might create a new sense of enthusiasm, even excitement, but probably only for awhile. I cannot conceive of OT having fewer or less severe objective dilemmas and challenges than OD.

So the cold, clear light of dawn will come sooner or later, however exuberant the present OT formulations.

The point can be made another way. Rechristening can create a sense of new and enlarged ownership, and that promises a useful check against OD in-groupiness and narrow protectionism. But there are ways to do that other than through alternative labels—ways in which OT and OD practitioners should be more versed than others, and ways that run less risks of we/they outcomes. Hence the call in an earlier Process Observer for a congress or synod or convocation to deal interactively with basic issues—of coverage, emphasis, technology, and values—such as those implied by the OT/OD interface. Rechristening more likely would disguise or even camouflage such basic issues than it would deal with them.

Notes

1. John D. Adams, ed., *Transforming Work* (Alexandria, Va.: Miles River Press, 1984).
2. The presentation was given to the OD Division at the 1984 annual meeting of the Academy of Management, in Boston.
3. Adams, *Transforming Work*, vii.
4. Ibid., viii–ix.

7

Some Differences between OD Generations, I: Four Generations and a Few Differentiae

Demographics matter: that is the basic notion proposed by this essay and its paired piece that follows. The general proposition comes as no surprise, of course, but the point has not been highlighted in OD. And this underemphasis justifies this piece and its partner. Together, they do four things. This piece tries its hand at identifying four OD generations, and sketches some differences in "basic orientations" between them. The partner piece provides complementary analysis of two other sets of differences between the four generations: in professional socialization; and in the general guides they rely on in professional life—their "lode stars."

The intent is to focus on "different from" rather than on two troublesome alternatives—"better than" or "worse than." No doubt, not all readers will agree that this intent dominates all of the time. The interpretive lenses of readers will differ; and no doubt my parochial preferences will seem to intrude, at least on occasion, clear intent notwithstanding. But so be it. I will try, hard, to respect my intentions as I work to realize the ambitions of this pair of essays.

The Generations

For openers, let us distinguish four OD generations which will provide context for the subsequent discussion. The generations are:

I *Founding fathers:* Bradford, Benne, Lippitt, and McGregor.
II *Few prominent recruits:* Argyris, Beckhard, Bennis, Blake, Buchanan, Dyer, Gibb, Schein, Schmidt, Shepard, Tannenbaum, and Thelen, most prominently.
III *An expanding network:* Blumberg, French, Friedlander, King, Margulies, Miles, Moffitt, Raia, Edie and Charlie Seashore, Walton, Worden, and myself, among others.
IV *Postinstitutionalization expansion:* Beer, Burke, Carrigan, Culbert, Goodstein, Nadler, Petrella, Porter, Vaill, and Weisbord, among others.

These four generations are not offered as either complete or comprehensive. Thus some might propose that Kurt Lewin belongs in Generation I, and who could deny the point, even though death struck him down well before the laboratory movement he helped sponsor led to the evolution of today's OD. Moreover, other later generations could easily be identified. However, four must suffice here. This is due not only to limitations of space but, in the present view, Generation III is like the first two generations while Generation IV serves to model those that have followed so far. For present limited purposes, then five generations would be too many and three too few.

What differences distinguish the two clusters of generations, at least for openers? Eight emphases focus on "different from" in this paper and its fraternal twin to follow. Here attention is directed at three generational differences that may be aggregated under a single heading:

Differences in basic orientations
- group process versus organizational content
- values versus technologies
- interaction/commitment versus accumulating knowledge and experience

"Some Differences Between OD Generations, II" will add detail about five other generational differences. For purposes of organizing, these five features will be classified as: differences in socialization; or differences in lode stars.

Differences in Basic Orientations

"Basic orientations" are doubtless more easily illustrated than defined. Three emphases do the illustrative job, for present purposes.

1. Process and product or content. Early OD generations were strong on "process" in small groups, often living with one's intervention successes or failures for weeks or even longer at a time, with the same group, and even occasionally with a co-trainer, where the probabilities of constructive feedback are high. Here, the trainer or consultant had a largely facilitative role, and client needs dominated. *The* early problem involved the translation of these attitudes and skills into large organizations. Here the early record contains much plain foolishness,[1] if often attractive and high-minded foolishness.

Later generations are distanced from this mix of opportunities/limitations. "Group process" is less the common denominator, in part because far fewer training venues exist. Moreover—to increase OD's relevance for coping with organizational issues, as well as to unabashedly add adherents—the emphasis swung toward organization "content": job enrichment, QWL, matrix organization, survey/feedback, even neurolinguistic programming in applications for negotiators seeking to be one-up, and so on.

To some degree, the distinction between process and product/content is not one that in practice either can be, or should be, maintained in extreme forms. For example, consider persons who learned about their strong preference for specific interpersonal and group processes, let us say in a T-group or a sensitivity training group. Quite reasonably, they might inquire: How can I approach such processes in my workday organizations? Purely process approaches provide incomplete and unsatisfactory answers. For example, our questioner might receive this piece of advice:

> Well, try to get other people in your organization to have a similar experience. Then those people, like yourself, will "seed" the organization. At some point, a "critical mass" will be achieved, and then appropriate changes in policies and procedures can be made by this enlightened cadre.

So what's "appropriate"? That's the rub. Such advice can be very frustrating. Thus it does not address the "what" of the specific structures and policies/procedures appropriate for OD processes. A purely process orientation could only fall back onto itself and note, elliptically, that characteristic OD values—openness, trust, and so on—would provide sufficient guides for whatever gets done. In this view, no "bad" policy or structural arrangements exist, only those which are inadequately supported by OD processes.

A "how" does not satisfy many intent on finding guidance about "what," however, for understandable reasons. Thus moderate observers can understand the desire to avoid reinventing the wheel, or inventing an awkward one. At the same time, those moderates recognize that it can be hard to distinguish such pragmatism from what is at base a desire for a "quick fix." The latter could undercut not only ownership and commitment, but also might encourage a succession of mindless organizational sheep-dips for those wanting to do it the "easy way."

Put directly, process *and* product or content provide the only reasonable emphases. And, at worst, this would have moderately challenged some features at the heart of classical OD: a dominantly facilitative role for the consultant, an emphasis on choice by the client rather than change, and a locating responsibility in the client.

To the degree that the issue became process *versus* product or content, however, this vital balance would move from the client model *toward* the expert model. At its worst, this could encourage clients to seek others to do for them that which they would not do for themselves, or perhaps even that for which they would not take direct responsibility.

Opinions differ in the degree to which it has been *and* or *versus* in OD. For example, Azzaretto concludes there has been far too much emphasis on process *versus* product or content, and he is definite that the latter has dominated the former. In addition, Azzaretto seems to question the legitimacy of process *and* product or content. In any case, his abstract notes:[2]

Early concepts of OD where practitioners facilitated the change process have recently given way to expert consultants directing the change through purposeful planning and systematic methodologies. The focus of many contemporary OD efforts is on the methods, techniques, or intervention approaches used to bring about the desired change.

The shift in the approach used by OD consultants from facilitating the change process to purposefully directing individual and organizational change has brought about confusion and trouble at the core of OD theory and practice.

2. Values and technologies. The drift toward product and content was heightened by, and reflected in, a corresponding deemphasis of concern about values by later OD generations. This drift has been sketched earlier in the contribution "Why OD?: Putting Values in their Prominent Place." So a brief characterization will suffice here.

Directly, not only is the "process" orientation quite value-specific, but most early ODers were preoccupied with the goal of creating new and better societies at work.[3] Technological spin-offs beyond the T-group were not mainstream, and the whole "learning design" approach was looked at in the early days with a jaundiced eye because it threatened diagnosis of specific sites, and perhaps especially because packaged designs violated group-process values prescribing *ad hoc* designs for specific interaction settings.

In later generations, value emphases often lurk in the shade of technological preoccupation, if anywhere. "Technology" is used loosely to encompass such a variety as team building, job enrichment, survey feedback, alpha/beta/gamma change, and so on. To be sure, this drift has been counterbalanced in part. The evolving "Statement of Values and Ethics . . ." for OD intervenors is one such useful across-the-grain effort, as are warnings about why and how eager and able technocrats can be set working in directions they neither recognize nor support.[4]

3. Commitment and accumulating knowledge. A third difference between OD generations aids and abets the two features sketched above. This third "basic orientation" can be sketched briefly, since it provides yet another perspective on a common theme.

Knowledge comes from both theory/experimentation and interaction, it seems obvious in the general case. Specifically, however, OD has been a poor switch-hitter. Early generations emphasized interaction and consequent commitment by specific individuals. Later generations are often concerned that this bias involves reliving history because of our failure to learn from it. They rely more on accumulating theory, and especially on learning packages that "worked" in similar settings.

Again, the issue is often framed—even if implicitly—as commitment *versus* cumulative knowledge. As such, this reinforces the reduced emphasis on process and on explicit values, since many are attracted to "cumulative knowledge" in one of two forms. Thus some are convinced that OD is in part a science and thus cumulative knowledge is both a useful product and a desired goal. Others respond more to the apparent shortcut provided by "cumulative knowledge," as in the reliance on canned designs that have worked elsewhere.

The job is not done yet: "Some Differences Between OD Generations, II" will add supporting detail and counterpoint.

But the basic conclusion seems emergent. OD's viable continuance will require both a past serving as a foundation and a future to extend and perhaps replace once essential parts of that foundation. This implies linkages between the generations, and the sketches above imply that making these linkages will require the best that is in us.

Notes

1. See the neglect of macro features in Warren G. Bennis and Philip Slater, "Democracy Is Inevitable," *Harvard Business Review* 42 (March 1964): 51–59. The tide turned, quickly. See Warren G. Bennis, "A Funny Thing Happened on the Way to the Future," *American Psychologist* 25 (July 1970): esp. 598–603.
2. John F. Azzaretto, "The Shift in OD From Process to Product," *Group and Organization Studies* 10 (Sept. 1985): 229.
3. This rootedness often was overt, as in the early works of the founding fathers. Moreover, the various "needs models" of Maslow, Argyris, and others in effect were normatively selective guides for OD intervenors, although their originators emphasized their humanistic character and touched but lightly (if at all) on the value implications of the needs.
4. See, for example, Ethan A. Singer and Leland M. Wooton, "The Triumph and Failure of Albert Speer's Administrative Genius," *Journal of Applied Behavioral Science* 12 (Jan. 1976): 79–103.

8

Some Differences between OD Generations, II: Socialization and Lode Stars

The preceding essay needs complementing. It provides a kind of manning chart of four OD generations, recall, which is repeated here as a convenience for the reader:

I *Founding fathers:* Bradford, Benne, Lippitt, and McGregor.
II *Few prominent recruits:* Argyris, Beckhard, Bennis, Blake, Buchanan, Dyer, Gibb, Schein, Schmidt, Shepard, Tannenbaum, and Thelen, most prominently.
III *An expanding network:* Blumberg, French, Friedlander, King, Margulies, Miles, Moffitt, Raia, Edie and Charlie Seashore, Walton, Worden, and myself, among others.
IV *Postinstitutionalization expansion:* Beer, Burke, Carrigan, Culbert, Goodstein, Nadler, Petrella, Porter, Vaill, and Weisbord, among others.

In addition, that earlier view of OD generations focused on differences in basic orientations, three of which got detailed attention. They directed attention at three features of the earlier OD generations: their emphases on group and personal processes, on values, and on interaction-based ownership and commitment by clients. In contrast, and especially for Generation IV, their emphases shifted toward—and in cases became dominated by—organizational products or outcomes, technology and learning designs or packages, as well as theory and accumulating knowledge.

This complementary essay focuses on two other sources of differences between the OD generations, and especially between the first three and the fourth. Thus one section below deals with difference in socialization, whose three illustrative features are sketched below as a preliminary to later discussion. And the second section introduces differences in lode stars, which contrast two basic guides to professional life characteristic of the two clusters of OD generations. In sum, this contribution to staking out major differences between OD generations will emphasize:

I Differences in socialization
- previous training and background
- rating and rejuvenation
- institutional bases for a new elite

II Differences in lode stars
- an elitism with populist tendencies versus a tempered populism with elitist tendencies
- OD marketplace as growing versus maturing

I   Differences in Socialization

Three differences in socialization selectively suggest sources of major incongruencies in the worldviews of the earlier and later OD generations. These incongruencies do not sharply separate the generations, but rather heighten intense dynamics of specific repulsion within a pattern of basic attraction.

1. Previous training and background.   The earliest OD generations were at once concentrated and diffuse. They were a small and basically academic elite, and were in that sense a concentrated band. Commonly, also most of the elders had independent scholarly reputations, and they often held tenure in traditional academic departments. They thus were often innovators with their overhead paid, from a revealing point of view. However, members of the first three generations came from all points of the substantive compass—from psychology, psychiatry, sociology, education, management, political science, and so on. So the early generations were diffuse in this crucial sense, as well as concentrated.

Beginning with the fourth generation identified above, its members had a profile that contrasts quite sharply with the cluster of earlier generations. Signally, the proportion of established academics drops precipitously. Generation IV was dominantly youngish, with careers of its members still in front of them. Academics among them came from a narrowing range of specialties, and some were even trained "in OD." But the bulk of the later generations, however credentialed, were in-house people working within the organizations they serviced. Moreover, they often were short timers, not only in the sense of being newly involved in OD but also because of short tours of duty in OD.

These two profiles are not optimally matched, to say the least. Rather, they imply major points of difference, if not abrasion.

2. Rating and rejuvenation.   The older OD generations faced a comfy environment. Their normal academic haunts were solidly reinforced for the small core by the "Bethel experience," in Maine as well as at several locations on the NTL circuit, and these common venues provided ample opportunity for skills to become known and developed, as well as for a recharging of the batteries to occur in the coming-together. Even our children became "NTL kids," looking forward to the summers in Maine. At their employing organizations, the identification of early generations with NTL was looked at as variously curious or even bizarre. But that sense of distinction, even if painful on occasion, on balance served to heighten the sense of belonging to a special and burgeoning social movement.

As NTL grew, this informal network lost credibility, due to a range of factors including the fact that many NTL members were deeply conflicted about rating or evaluation, especially of a formal kind. In brief, during the late 1960s and early 1970s—exacerbated by the retirement of NTL head Lee Bradford, an economic recession that sharply cut attendance at NTL offerings, and a key legal suit brought by a participant—NTL was torn asunder as it stood poised on the brink of what it might have become. In large part, this was due to *the* NTL dilemma: a giver of programs, whose practical face could conflict sharply with quality control, as when a major source of enrollments sought to influence selection of staff, or to *become* staff. Reinforced by the sometimes monumental counterdependence of some members, NTL shied away from accreditation even as it retained a selection process for a deliberately restricted network of colleagues.

As a consequence, those in Generation IV had a disjointed entry into their professional worlds. They typically had one foot more or less firmly planted in NTL, which was widely perceived as a sinking ship. And the other foot searched uncertainly for a toehold in the future. Both rating and rejuvenation had become quite problematic, and new institutions had to be developed.

3. OD institutions.   For the old generations, "who you were" was determined in two basic ways: by what you wrote, mostly in the traditional (and often staid) sources; and what you did "in group" and on sensitivity training staffs, usually for NTL but increasingly for various NTL colonies in the world—TRW, or Alcan, or whatever. One's efforts were visible to the small core, and quite opaque to those who could not be accommodated in the inner halls. In this regard, NTL was its own worst enemy. It turned on many more than could find a satisfying place at the main table, as it were.

ODers had to invent new ways to rate and rejuvenate. Consider only the International Association of Applied Social Scientists (IAASS), OD Network, and the OD Institute. They constitute the prime alternatives from which the new model for rating and rejuvenation will be drawn, with the eventual choice or combination still in doubt.

Many of the older generations who did not reject certification on principle saw IAASS as *the* reference group, especially because of its quality-control mandate. NTL was to be the "program arm" which provided rejuvenating assignments at attractive venues, while IAASS provided the certification of individuals. IAASS (now Certified Consultants International) never came on like a rushing wind, however. This was true even for the older generations and more definitely applies to Generation IV and beyond.

OD Network became *the* major reference association, in size and in enthusiasm. Its focus was quite definitely on rejuvenation rather than rating, however, with a high fun factor for a volatile and mass membership. ODN's quality-control activities are located in the gung-ho local groups that organize the ODN "happenings"—once held twice yearly, and now annually—with some tethering by a national board.

Put moderately, quality control was characterized far more by "y'all come" than by a desire to separate sheep from goats. Perhaps most prominently, ODN successfully sought male/female parity in its membership, and was otherwise basically hospitable to a very broad range of interests. Overall, ODN reflects a quite elastic concept of "OD." In contrast to both NTL and IAASS (or CCI), it has mass-membership features and no aspirations beyond providing a comfortable meeting group for a very broad range of people and perspectives. Those are reasonble and laudable aspirations, of course. But they do not focus on quality control.

The OD Institute falls somewhere between NTL and ODN. By and large, its membership is from later OD generations; however, ODI reflects a growing concern about quality control. ODI's 15-year history of nurturance by Don Cole has seen it grow from miniscule to modest size only, and it still firmly bears the mark of its founder. In contrast, NTL may well be said to be in its third generation of leadership, at a minimum, not counting temporary stewards. In addition, ODI has strong international outreaches and ambitions, which characterize NTL a bit but ODN hardly at all.

II Differences in Lode Stars

Two lode stars have guided OD travelers, as it were. Differences in these two major orienting biases help explain the historical myopia in OD, as well as the unconnectedness between generations.

1. Elitist/populist combinations. Early OD generations tended toward elitism, for reasons clearly implied in their basic orientation and socialization. But the elitism was leavened with populist tendencies. In useful contrast, later generations tempered populism with elitist tendencies. The early NTL and ODN, respectively, typify the two sets of combinations.

The implied tensions between generations could have been moderated only with awesome good luck. Movements get started by zealots with a sense of their uniqueness, and most movements reflect acute generational angst as they grow into complex and variously concretized realities. If nothing else, the replacement of "great leaders" is fraught with conflicting passions—admiration for the founding role, spiced by the need to find one's place among a rapidly expanding cohort of possible competitors. These conflicts characterize growing movements, and these virtually inevitables were exacerbated in OD's case by the economic downturn of the late 1960s which coincided with concerns about successors to Generation I.

2. *Different marketplaces.* For early generations, basically I through III, demand outstripped supply for quite a few years. Signally, few organizations had even a handful of the new breed on their own staffs. So early ODers often did not have to scuffle for business, in part because the substantial majority of early OD generations had independent programs of research that required time and tending. Indeed, if anything, *the* problem was to avoid overcommitting, which disease has shown up in physical and emotional shutdowns in a noteworthy proportion of the older OD generations.

Things changed, quite suddenly, for those in Generation IV and their successors. Momentously, on the supply side, large numbers of OD aspirants began appearing—let us say, in 1968–70. This inspired the concern of many among the earlier generations for quality control—of what OD was, who did it, and how. Newer generations tended toward opposite persuasions, in part due to immediate self-interests that contrasted with those of the elders. Later generations lacked enthusiasm for IAASS/CCI accreditation, for example, but often developed deep attachments to ODN, which required only a small fee but cultivated infectious enthusiasm in would-be members.

Developments on the demand side did not diminish these sources of differences, and often of contention. About 1968–70, the OD market experienced an extended plateau and probably a decline. Indeed, Krell[1] sees OD as a "mature market"—i.e., one with a substantial and growing supply of service providers for a demand that is stable or not increasing very much. The variously sober and shrill demands for quality control escalated just as the market "matured," and Krell proposes that the two events are not serendipitous. "Maturing markets" are characterized more by price competition than concern for quality, by "milking" rather than research and development, and by inflated claims and some disregard for realities. For new generations, especially, this environment was poorly suited to a transforming concern with standards, with enhancing practitioner skills, or with sharpening the focus of what OD is and is not. For the older hands, the same conditions encouraged not only a clamor for standards but also for certification and licensing.

Depending upon where you sat, then, the same activity could be differently interpreted. Old hands could pride themselves on preserving the essentials of their long march, while newer hands could read only or mostly a desire to restrict entry into an exciting and—the point had a growing salience—

financially rewarding line of work. This possibility discouraged a linking of the generations, in cases even linking between the generations.

These and other supply-and-demand dynamics no doubt contributed to generational differences, then. One can appreciate how more established ODers, especially, might have concerns about quality control. To be sure, a vocal segment of the older generations denied that anyone should have either the right or power to influence in/out decisions about potential ODers. Their grounds ranged widely—from high principle and abstract logic all the way (which may not be very far in cases!) to blatant counterdependence, fueled in many cases by real or imagined sleights in NTL or IAASS.

So the situation was more complicated than earlier paragraphs imply, but the general point holds nonetheless. Such supply-and-demand dynamics can exert powerful conditioning and divisive forces on the generations. Let me choose only a single contrast, and perhaps an unfair one. I recall my own NTL internship as a series of vibrant colors: the golden promises of a better tomorrow implied by the laboratory approach; the somber hues of concern about where all this might lead; the reddish tones associated with the risk and even danger of our new thing to a flowering personal career in one of the classic disciplines; and the imperial-purplish sense of joining a behavioral-science aristocracy, albeit a tiny remnant that once had to work hard to attract even a few network members.

My personal chromatograph was jumping all over the place, in short.

For the generation of NTL interns only about a decade removed from mine, their chromatographs were encouraged to have a very specific sensitivity. I recall the opening session of one group of my successors, with their lead-facilitator telling them how it was in the world they were about to enter. He encouraged the interns to think of color in connection with their upcoming experiences, but of a single hue: green. To underscore his point, our friendly helper waved an American bill—$100, I believe. And the facilitator reminded the aspirants that, while it would be "mucho" green for those who "made it," the realities favored the survival of only the fittest few, the competition being what it was for legitimation in the network.

III   Whither the Differences?

And so it goes with differences between the OD generations. Additional features might be added, but the net effect would remain basically unchanged.

So what can be made of the brief descriptions of contrasts between generations in this piece and its earlier partner? An area alive with inquiry may be said to have a vital central core and an active periphery, to hazard one perspective. Generational differences challenge and undercut this central core, and the danger seems to be intellectual gridlock if not schism.

Must these dynamics simply unwind themselves in some already determined way? I believe not, at least not necessarily. "Crosswalks," for example, can be built between the generations, that would cushion the historic and episodic differences. Other essays in this series introduce some of these crosswalks. Among others, please note the essays dealing with the values underlying OD, the statement of professional ethics, as well as the raising of consciousness about generational differences attempted by this pair of efforts.

Note

1. Terence C. Krell, "The Marketing of Organization Development," *Journal of Applied Behavioral Science* 17 (July 1981): 309–23.

9

Two Faces of OD:
Populism and Elitism

Organization Development results from the confluence of many lines of inquiry and thought—all centering on choice and change, and generally guided by ideals about growing participation and involvement. In this sense, OD can be thought of as having two major components: a relatively homogeneous and stable central core; and an outer fringe of approaches, techniques, and perspectives—some quite permanent, and others that come and go as fashions change and as perceived utilities dictate.

This core/fringe metaphor suggests two basic dynamics. The first is a constructive one—a building on shared territory, with time and experience determining when the building is on foundations that prove more hopeful than solid. The second dynamic emphasizes contention or dispute. OD is a composite, not some pure form, and will continue to add outer fringes to the central core. This heterogeneity implies the need to direct energy at determining when additions are complementary and when they are undercutting.

It requires only a little thought to envision conditions under which these dynamics could well serve the purposes of planned change, but just as obvious are the conditions under which the dynamics are self-defeating. The focus here is on one illustration of this basic duality in OD. This essay illustrates the two envisioned conditions, and suggests how the first might be encouraged and the second be made less likely.

The focus is on populism and elitism as they coexist in OD.

Some people might not like the word, but "populism" reflects a theme at the heart of OD. The emphasis will vary for different ODers, of course, but central features of OD thought and history provide a firm basis for the present characterization. The profession sprang from efforts to improve the life-chances of democratic systems, for one thing. And OD has a clear preference for broadening participation and involvement, which certainly are major components of any populist orientation.

At the same time, OD has a definite elitist streak, even a dominant one. In part, OD did not simply appear in the inventory of social commentary and science. It was proposed by champions, who were (or became) central figures. Like all social moments, then, OD had to deal with its internal elitism—typically forged in the crucible of lean times at start-up, and tempered by the flames of criticism from various external elites. Moreover, OD has a research orientation, which implies a degree of intellectual elitism among aficionados.

In short, OD was not nourished by Everyman, even as this technology-cum-values always has had strong liberation aspirations. Indeed, OD was nourished by various establishments—ESSO (now EXXON), the National Education Association, and so on. Indeed, perhaps the major stock criticism of OD proposes that its proponents are simply mouthpieces for the establishments who pay their fees, which can be substantial.

One does not have to be a weatherman to forecast what can happen with such strong winds blowing in opposite directions. A central point of conflict between elitist and populist tendencies in OD involved *the* classic issue: Who is in? And who is out? In OD's earliest days, settling such questions revolved around whether an individual was chosen as an intern and then as a fellow with the National Training Laboratory, or NTL. That defined being "in."

Elitists have no trouble with selection, in principle, given that practical choices might pose vexing trade-offs. Careful selection was necessary to keep the NTL flame alive. Hence the emphasis on talent and competence for NTL members, as these were variously defined. At the same time, as a practical matter, certain cases in doubt might be decided positively, because a certain potential member had various advantages—a powerful supporting cohort, access to new business, or whatever. Prudently responding to such advantages also could help keep the NTL flame alive.

The populist orientation had a lot of trouble with selecting in/out, however. Who was to say what the criteria were? Moreover, how could NTL stand for what it said it said it stood for, and bar the gates for *any* enthusiastic would-be members? NTL political accommodations, real and imagined, added substantial heat and intensity to such earnest questioning.

The contention did not cease when NTL surrendered the certification arena to the International Association of Applied Social Scientists, which—for reasons of an awkward acronym, among others—not only became Certified Consultants International, but more recently moderated its role in the OD certification business. The contention about elitism/populism helps explain—at least to me—why IAASS, which became CCI, apparently seeks to downplay that troublesome business.

Personally, I do not have much of a problem with the elitist and populist tendencies, as long as the parties keep talking to one another. In large part, this may be due to my failure—if that is what it is—to decide on how I wish to be known in regard to elitism/populism. My way of viewing myself encompasses the duality and seeks to live with the real tensions. Firmly, I see myself as an elitist with real and even strong populist tendencies.

Now, is that some titillating play on words? What can it mean to be an elitist with populist tendencies? Let me provide two illustrations.

1. The general case.   At several points in these essays—in "OD as Increasing Responsible Freedom in Organization," for example—I refer to the tension between populist and elitist orientations. I see far too much unnecessary repression in most organizations, which of course reflects the populist in me. At the same time, I am convinced that this repression cannot simply be willed away, and even less can it be revolutionized away. Nobody's will is that strong; and revolutions—except for the unique American experience, as I read history—are better for replacing one oppressive regime with another than they are for eliminating repression. So the pragmatist in me—some would say it is the elitist—fixates on this key question: If not what we have now, *then what?*

Populists often cringe at this question, but their tocsins—e.g., Power to the people, now—do not chart a program. Such slogans can help "circulate" the elite, of course, and this can be refreshing in itself. But "circulation" provides no program for action.

Even in the presence of firm programs, of course, new elites have the distressing habit of quickly coming to act like the old elite they replaced. But articulated programs seem to me nonetheless useful and, indeed, necessary.

So I have geared myself for the very long run, committed to the search for specific organizational alternatives that not only increase personal freedom and satisfaction but that also tend to have positive objective consequences. The latter include the usual list—heightened productivity, lower waste, better quality, and so on—as well as those cases in which enhancements in personal freedom come at little or no cost to the employing organization. The intent is obvious: to move toward greater personal freedom, in quite explicit ways, that are also relatively safe in that those ways contribute to both broadly social needs as well as to narrower economic considerations.

That's how I integrate my selves: an elitist with definite and even strong populist tendencies. This does not strike me as at all curious. Indeed, this rolling duality seems necessary to me, as well as comfortable for me. Only an elitist can have the time and support necessary to focus on the long-run search for organizational alternatives; and, at present, only elites (both union and management) can consistently authorize this search and especially applications of its products. Simultaneously, populist contributions loom large. Typically, one learns only because many in organizations variously contribute their time, talent, and trust. On occasion, even in my limited experience such contributions have involved substantial personal risk to organization members. Moreover, no matter how elegant an OD design and its supporting research, it can never apply itself.

So here I sit, perhaps copping-out on the populist revolution even as I keep a substantial distance from several elites, but intentionally and determinedly trying to contribute to both.

There are costs, of course, but I find them bearable. Being in-between—or "marginal" in the sociologist's terminology—is at once enriching and empowering in general, even as in specifics it can cause concern about "whose side you are on, anyway?"

Difficulties can arise, then, as when an attracive contract is lost. But I try to be balanced about the matter; and my general observation is that both parties are better off after a parting of the ways, especially when that happens early in the game. Moreover, the OD role is a marginal one—with one's feet in several cultures simultaneously—and failure to "get it" occasionally from all sides would lead me to be concerned that I was doing something basically wrong.

In any case, I feel good that my duality has not been a cop-out. We are not yet ready to leap to a new world of work, but we have an increasingly clear view of some of the specifics that can help in moving us in that direction. Over the years, my colleagues and I have helped "make the match"— meeting individual needs and organization demands—in several particular cases, of which I highlight a few:

- the 3-Dimensional Image design for mutual learning by conflictful or noncollaborative pairs of individuals or groups[1]
- changes in organization culture by means of laboratory learning and interaction-centered designs[2]
- the demotion design, as an alternative to firing satisfactory performers during economic crunches[3]
- the use of flexible work-hours programs to aid both employees and their managers[4]
- the conceptual elaboration of a plural model of change to help assess degree and kind of change[5]
- the elaboration of how various structural models and policy variations can help meet OD goals,[6] both in support of, as well as in preparation for, interaction-centered designs

- estimating success rates of OD applications—in the Western world,[7] as well as in developing countries[8] and economically deprived settings[9]—with the goal of motivating other and more extensive applications
- the measurement and amelioration of stress or burnout at work[10]

2. A specific case.   Dwelling on personal experience is not unpleasant, but broader vistas also reflect the populist/elitist duality, and also suggest its benefits. A dramatic case of elitist <---> populist interaction comes from Bombay,[11] where a volunteer group provided the survey skills necessary to help establish some facts relevant to the well-being of Bombay street dwellers, whose collaboration permitted and facilitated the application of the technical skills.

The local government operated on the basis of some convenient assumptions about street dwellers, who exist under incredibly trying circumstances, and unrealistic public policies were legitimated by these assumptions. For example, public policy assumed that by and large street dwellers had drifted into Bombay from distant rural provinces and were in a sad, but nonetheless temporary, status, as well as one that was better than the far away conditions they had left. Both assumptions encourage feeble public responses. As migrants from afar, went one rationalization, the street dwellers could hardly expect the treatment appropriate for locals. Why should locals pay for the failures of distant governments, moreover, who in effect exported what should have been a problem handled at home? In addition, their assumedly temporary status as street dwellers implied a kind of invisible hand that "solved" the problem even as their numbers grew.

Reality testing of such assumptions required technical means to isolate and highlight their truth-value. The street dwellers could hardly field and interpret a survey, but they could (and did) come to understand its potential and cooperate with it, in ways considered out of the question for people so preoccupied with the bare essentials of everyday living.

Findings of the survey were arresting in numerous regards. Consider only two particulars. The bulk of street dwellers were from the local state, not some far-off jurisdiction pouring its problems into Bombay. Moreover, street dwelling was hardly temporary, with some 40 percent of the population surveyed having been born on the streets of Bombay.

Public policy might become no more benign. But never again could it take the old and convenient pathways. Moreover, consciousness was raised among street dwellers; and consciences may have been pricked in more affluent quarters. Those are prime components of new public policies.

Epilogue

So, come on, future! OD is getting ready for you, both in its elitist and populist manifestations.

Notes

1. Robert T. Golembiewski and Arthur Blumberg, "Training and Relational Learning: The Confrontation Design." *Training and Development Journal* 21 (Nov. 1967): 35–43.
2. Robert T. Golembiewski and Stokes B. Carrigan, "Planned Change in Organization Style Based on Laboratory Approach," *Administrative Science Quarterly* 15 (March 1970): 79–93; "The Persistence of Laboratory-Induced Changes in Organization Styles," *Administrative Science Quarterly*, 15 (Sept. 1970): 330–40.
3. Robert T. Golembiewski, Stokes B. Carrigan, Walter R. Mead, Robert F. Munzenrider, and Arthur Blumberg, "Toward Building New Work Relationships," *Journal of Applied Behavioral Science* 8 (March 1972): 135–48.
4. Robert T. Golembiewski, Richard Hilles, and Munro Kagno, "A Longitudinal Study of Flexi-Time Effects: Some Consequences of an OD Structural Intervention," *Journal of Applied Behavioral Science* 10 (Dec. 1974): 503–32.
5. Robert T. Golembiewski, Keith Billingsley, and Samuel Yeager, "Measuring Change and Persistence in Human Affairs," *Journal of Applied Behavioral Science* 12 (June 1976): 133–57.
6. Robert T. Golembiewski, *Approaches to Planned Change*. New York: Marcel Dekker, 1979, vol. 2.
7. Robert T. Golembiewski, Carl W. Proehl, Jr., and David Sink, "Estimating the Success of OD Applications," *Training and Development Journal* 72 (April 1982): 86–95.
8. Robert T. Golembiewski, "Is OD Narrowly Culture-Bound?: Prominent Features of 100 Third-World Applications," *Organization Development Journal* 5 (Winter 1987): 86–95.
9. Robert T. Golembiewski, "OD Applications under Economic Deprivation," *Public Administration Quarterly* (in press).
10. Robert T. Golembiewski, Richard Hilles, and Rick Daly, "Some Effects of Multiple OD Interventions on Burnout and Worksite Features," *Journal of Applied Behavioral Science* 23 (Dec. 1987): 295–314.
11. The Society for Participatory Research in Asia, New Delhi, India, prepared this survey, largely with volunteers. For the underlying model, see the Society's *Knowledge and Social Change*, Oct. 1985.

10

OD's Near-Term Destiny: Professional Maturation or Time's Dumpster?

OD is "controversial" in some circles nowadays, and that implies good news as well as bad. A healthy and expanding field should at once stimulate emphases on differences and deficiencies, as well as be stimulated by them. Clearly, however, limits exist. Hence some observers are worried that in OD too much is being made of a good thing. Thus McLean and his associates observe: ". . . the current fasion seems to require increasingly emphatic and colourful assertions of [OD] demise. It is as if some people are competing to find better ways of denouncing OD."[1]

The change in fashion clearly encompasses a great range. Not too long ago we were reading mostly about "the coming death of bureaucracy," and even brave if vague assertions that organizational "democracy is inevitable" excited the hopeful. The prognoses have shifted, however, definitely and decidedly. I recently reviewed one submission to a scholarly journal whose subtitle proclaimed: "OD Sucks." More moderately, so far has the fashion of negativism apparently taken hold, that unexpected results often get interpreted even by careful observers as "challenging OD's fundamentals"[2] when less-sweeping explanations clearly exist that are at least equally satisfying,[3] if not more so.

How to interpret this drop in popularity ratings? Some see OD as heading toward time's short-term dumpster, like the refuse from some New Year's Eve party. In effect, in this view, OD was fun while it lasted. But it left somebody with a lot of cleaning up to do, and it produced hangovers of regret or disappointment in others.

Consider an opposite view. If we don't weaken, not only is the counteraction understandable, but it reflects substantial past progress more than future despair, and perhaps paramountly it provides the vehicle necessary for continuing professional maturation. The validity of this approach fetches powerful reinforcement from what seems in the past few years a definite reversal of earlier pessimism, may the reader please note. It seems too soon to baptize this reversal as the next major trend; nor can one say confidently how far the reversal will continue. But it seems sensible to conclude that the strongest negative reactions have been heard, and responded to with a considerable degree of effect.

Let us settle here for supporting the reasonableness of this second interpretation, while leaving for others the issue of whether the anticipated effects already have occurred. Four points suggest the fuller argument supporting both the reasonableness of a counter reaction and its benign potential, *if* ODers do not lose heart.

First, the early hopes or expectations about OD needed tethering. The world has been whirling for awhile now, and its momentum is not easily or casually disturbed. A delicate balance is required, and that balance involves two features: acknowledging that awesome momentum and also that entropy has all the trump cards, while resolutely heightening the search for longer and more effective levers to move behavior and relationships from accustomed orbits. Incautious enthusiasm dominated early, and expectations typically skidded beyond the balance point.

A correction was past due, and we should not interpret the necessary and desirable as some portent of imminent doom. The medicine will only help ODers, if they will take it for what it is.

Second, early OD emphasized the nice things—integration, growth, truth/love, and so on. This bias needed complementing by reasonable attention to disagregation, decay, and power/coercion, if OD's range were to be extended to match social and economic realities. Such crucial extensions have significant costs, of course—potential conflicts between values, developing a larger portfolio of skills and learning designs, and (more generally) really understanding that both sun and rain make flowers grow, with too much of either being the real problem.

Again, highlighting the condition points to the need for correction, not its impossibility. Power/coercion does not necessarily diminish the salience of truth/love,[4] but provides a context for it while posing challenges that need to be faced.

Third, the stakes needed raising about what was considered tolerable performance in interventions as well as in research. Much progress has been made on this point. Failures have been documented; and constraints hedging overreliance on such learning vehicles as the T-Group became clearer. The key point here involves being clear that the revisionist research and experience focus on deviant cases rather than reject fundamentals.

Ample evidence implies that OD has a respectable batting average, even as the revisionist literature rightly points to failures in practice and to gaps in theory. See three subsequent pieces in this volume—"So, What about Success Rates?" and "You Can't be a Beacon," I and II—which seek to show that the revisionist literature points up areas for improvement rather than denies attractive success rates, thank you, even as a definite margin for improvement does exist. What is fundamental and what is marginal have to be kept firmly in mind. Again, the problem is in the interpretation rather than in the results of the revisionist literature.

Fourth, the founding OD gurus deserve respect, but no claims to infallability ever were appropriate. Hence critical examination even of core OD notions always has a priority and, almost of necessity, this induces tensions between founding and succeeding generations. Such generational dynamics are always difficult, and can be untidy. At best, succeeding generations demand an independent assay, and inevitably will find dross and even some fool's gold. At worst, the generations will really gap—and "eating of the guru" occurs, if you will, inducing resentment in one party and discomfort or even guilt in the other. Good will, sensitivity, and graciousness can avoid the worst, although the job will not be an easy one. For some perspective on the challenges associated with generational gaps *at their most benign*, see "Some Differences Between OD Generations," I and II.

So the current and immediately past tensions in OD—even the occasional signs of nastiness—are more an expected dynamic than a sign of the final days. Recall the Polish proverb: Success always has a thousand parents, and failure forever remains an orphan.

So enough examples, already. Commonly, they all have Janus-like features. The examples suggest the need for counterreactions which, technically and especially emotionally, can be interpreted as either signaling progress for OD, or implying the death of OD.

Only two things seem relatively certain. Thus one's tendency to see demise versus progress depends on personal judgments as to whether the four illustrative points are "normal" and "expected" in the evolution of any field. Those illustrations seem unexceptional to me, based on my sense of the experience in both the physical and behavioral sciences.

Moreover, and a far more important certainty, we can bias the progress versus demise outcome, to some unknown but probably substantial degree, by our going-in assumptions. So why not interpret the present orientation as "progress?" That may prove wrong, to be sure. But if we prefer to see "demise," that will only speed the day and time when what we expect will occur, in part because our expectations encourage that outcome. Indeed, those expectations may in fact determine that outcome.

Notes

1. A. J. McLean, D. B. Sims, I. L. Mangham, and D. Tuffield, *Organization Development in Transition* (New York: Wiley, 1982), 121.
2. Jerry I. Porras and Alan Wilkins, "Organization Development in Large System," *Journal of Applied Behavioral Science* 16 (Dec. 1980): 506–34.

3. Robert T. Golembiewski, "Isolating Some Elements of Victory from Defeat Too Easily Acknowledged," *Journal of Applied Behavioral Science* 18 (Nov. 1, 1982): 143–48.
4. For example, see Melvin Le Baron, "New Perspectives Toward More Effective Local Elected Councils and Boards," 235–53, in Robert T. Golembiewski and William Eddy, eds, *Organization Development in Public Administration* (New York: Marcel Dekker, 1977), vol. 2.

11

The Yellow Envelope on the Floor: Does Paying the Piper Imply Calling the Tune?

It was a dramatic scene, in an apparently unobtrusive way. The casual observer might sense only a bit of untidiness, but those in the know were at once wary and aware of what was at general issue.

The scene? Visualize the sitting room in a comfortable hotel suite, and focus on the green-carpeted floor. More or less smack-dab in the middle of the central open space is an envelope, bright yellow. If you focus on that envelope, and if your eyesight is more or less normal, you do not have to get very close to see a bold legend, in capital letters:

DR. ROBERT GOLEMBIEWSKI

CONSULTANT

Now imagine time-lapse photography of that sitting room covering a period of five or so hours. People enter the suite, and react in a similar way. They pause, and then move toward that envelope—as toward some known object. And then they veer away, as if repelled. Many people enter the suite in that half-day, but the envelope remains—not only in place, but unremarked although observed by all.

I write "observed by all," but that may overstate the case. Certainly, I knew about it, and so did my host-client—let's call him Tom, although that is not his name. Indeed, he had deposited the envelope there . . . but I get ahead of my story.

So two of us definitely knew about that envelope, and tolerated that knowledge—each knowing the other knew, but both allowing the envelope to lay throughout a long day of closely scheduled appointments.

If "observed by all" does overstate the case, however, it is not by much. The common flight path of our visitors permits no other conclusion. The people—coming through the suite that day recognized the envelope at a distant glance: it was the kind their organization uses for nonpayroll checks such

52

as those for expenses, consultants, and the like. And hence they were attracted to it. Perhaps this came from mere curiosity, but I suspect most initially approached with an interest in helping. But as they got close enough to see the addressee they knew that something was at stake other than carelessness or inadvertence. Hence, to a person, our visitors veered away swiftly.

Our visitors were correct in their general wariness, and that is no surprise. For rising to positions of influence in the organization whose envelope lay on the floor—and all our visitors had so risen—requires great sensitivity, and far more than average caution and hunkering down under uncertainty. Indeed, several of our visitors reconstructed the essential dynamics between my host and myself, dynamics that led to the yellow envelope getting on the carpet in the middle of the open space, and remaining there for hours.

What were the high points of those dynamics? My host had sponsored a set of team-building experiences for those reporting to him as well as those in his broader organization, and it had been a rough experience for him. He had been forewarned that the processes might sting, for he was in trouble with his staff, and for reasons that he substantially created and perpetuated. But his need was great, and he was (in his own words) a "bigger boy than most." So we went ahead, with my usual team-building format:[1] individual interviews to diagnose the local conditions; a feedback session for all to sketch a possible design and to discuss the probability of success, given the diagnosis; and then a go/no-go decision, subject to a veto by either the supervising executive or by a number of subordinates, operationally defined as "more than 15 to 20 percent" who had strong concerns about going ahead.

The design to go ahead was unanimous, with the executive urging: "It's now or never. Let's see if they have the stomach to take me on."

His subordinates took him at his word, and even recommended more than once over several days of energetic discussion that he consider resignation as the only remedy. The executive was shocked and hurt. He alternated between seeing his subordinates as "ingrates," in the main, and as "gutless" for having held back so much and so long.

Nonetheless, quite specific contracts were hammered out, and usefully so, I concluded.

And now we were back to hold updating sessions with all participants. Individual contracts would be reviewed on our first day. Then a combined meeting would be held over the following two days—basically for looking forward, but with some early attention to reviewing the immediate past.

The executive and I met an hour or so before the first session with one of his first reports, and we both agreed that things had gone well after the team sessions. "Tough, and not uniformly upbeat, but necessary," we both agreed.

"And how about you?" I inquired in several cycles. "You took your lumps. Any unfinished business?"

"I'm great," he responded. "You know I'm a bigger boy than most."

But there seemed to be at least one snake in the grass. A minute or two before the first scheduled arrival—who would be on time, you could set your watch by it—the executive walked over to his briefcase. "Oh, by the way, I stopped by our controller's office to get your check." I prepared to say something bright, but had no chance.

"Here's your blood money," the executive announced. And he tossed the envelope in my direction. It had no chance to reach me, and fluttered to the floor—face up, as fate would have it—perhaps 10 to 15 feet from me.

We looked at one another—without speaking, as I recall—for a few seconds, and then came the knock on the door. Our first appointment had arrived. "Come on in, the door's open," we both said, more or less in unison. Our first appointment zigged toward the envelope, about equidistant between the executive and myself. And then he zagged. "Good to see you again, Bob," he said while extending his hand. "Let's get to work on our contract."

More or less, the scene was repeated throughout the day, as individual first reports came by for their one-on-one session with their boss to check on progress. I was the facilitator.

Our last one-on-one session finished, we had time to devote to our unfinished business. The first reports would soon be back as a group, for drinks and dinner, but we did have a break of an hour or so.

"We should talk about the envelope," the executive noted. "If we don't, my fantasy is that my guys will hug the walls when they come in. They know the business is between us, and I guess they're waiting for a signal from us that we've either got things square or we need their help."

"I suspect that," he added, "since you didn't pick up the envelope all during the day, you're not predisposed to ever pick it up. So, I suppose, if I don't pick it up, it'll stay there."

"Not so," I replied. "I'll be pleased to pick it up, and also to deposit it to my account. With three kids in private colleges, I know what to do with the money!"

"But," I added by way of qualification, "let's both be clear on why that yellow envelope lays where it does."

So we talked.

We covered some important miles together in the next 90 minutes or so. Let me abstract that discussion, which was sufficiently "finished" that evening for me to pick up the check, and for the check thrower and I to embrace after I did.

The territory we covered in our talk related to the limits on a folk saying: Who pays the piper calls the tune.

The sense of our talk was direct. In OD, that saying has very sharp limits. Paying implies something, of course, but one can easily make too much of reasonable (and even good) things.

Several commonalities emerged from the discussion. They will be reviewed in outline form, which conveys the substance even as it underplays the emotionality. But so be it.

1. We agreed that anger precipitated the throwing of the check. The team building had jarred the executive, and his emotions had been suppressed. Much to his surprise, they propelled him into an impulsive act. He thought his defenses were stouter, and his self-control greater. He did not remember using the term "blood money."

2. Throwing the check was not premeditated, but the symbolism was quickly clear to both of us. The act was both an attack on me, and a test. If I simply picked up the check, I would be damned for what I did as a facilitator, and stamped as one whose future actions the executive could control providing he bid higher than the others.

3. Picking up the check at the controller's office was an unusual act for the executive, but his conscious thought had been to express his thanks for my help in team building.

4. The first reports probably had a good sense of what the yellow envelope on the carpet signified. The executive was known as having a strong need to "get even."

5. I could not have picked up the check, even if I wanted, after the initial first report entered the suite. The word no doubt would have spread that I valued mammon more than process.

6. The executive could not pick up the check during the day, in part due to his own turbulent feelings and in part because he felt "the ball was in my court, for good or ill."

7. Both of us were worried: he because of an act he saw as impetuous, even demeaning; and I because of what I may have communicated that encouraged such an act or, worse still, that gave the executive the sense that I might grovel for my fee.

8. We thought the one-on-one sessions went very well. The check *was* on the floor, but we both had sufficient trust that we would get to it when time permitted. And it would take some time, so we let the envelope lay.

So it went, and we were still in deep discussion when the first reports began to arrive. Quickly, expectantly, we were all there.

"You guys want to talk about a yellow envelope?" the executive began.

"You bet," came the general reply. One attendee added: "We have learned to trust enough to wait, but we also need to process this one before my trust account is empty."

Discussion took a direct tack. One attendee explained: "Two months ago, that envelope would have stopped us cold. But I just knew we would learn from it, when we had process time. The envelope got my attention but, hell, you guys seemed to carry right on. After a while, I forgot about the damned envelope, and the check I knew was in it. But I remembered as I left the room, and took an arabesque around it!"

These reflect some of the specifics of what is general issue, and sometimes becomes momentous. That involves drawing the line concerning what the payer can reasonably expect when it comes to calling the tune the OD specialist will play.

Note

1. Details of the entry design appear elsewhere. Basically, that design seeks to diagnose "conflict of agreement" or "conflict of disagreement," and to predict the probable effects of the appropriate design. See Robert T. Golembiewski, *Approaches to Planned Change*. (New York: Marcel Dekker 1979), vols. 1 and 2.

12

Is OD Universalistic or Particularistic? Some Similarities between Private- and Public-Sector Consultation*

Interstitial or marginal persons often get what they deserve, for their common range is a treacherous one: from threatened poaching, to opining that "your baby sure is ugly." Nonetheless, as is my habit, I find myself again exploring an interface, or the lack thereof.

So perhaps I should show my colors, as it were, and early. I feel I am reasonably situated to have opinions on the issue of contextual differences/similarities in consultation. Thus I spend part of my academic year helping staff a public management program at the University of Georgia; and I apply a good chuck of time to the affairs of the faculty of what is essentially a Canadian school of business, albeit with some generic inclinations. In addition, my publications fall in roughly equal thirds, by general orientation: more or less explicitly public, business, and generic. And I actively work both sides of the consulting street, though more frequently and more profitably (in terms of opportunities to innovate and to couple research with consultation, as well as financially) in business contexts.

Let me also be explicit about my biases. I recognize these days are not hospitable to interstitials. Many of those in public management find themselves in a defensive posture in the face of aggressive efforts at bureaucrat bashing and of blizzards of proposals for privatization of various sorts. And their basic defense is: Public management *is* different, really. Some careless pro–public-management folk have even come perilously close to finding conceptual comfort in a neotraditional politics versus administration duality, and this after strenuous and long-lasting demonstrations that these two realms—sometimes distinguished as value versus fact—are intermingled in all organizations. The motivation for this neoclassicism? The more one can differentiate "public" from "business," the less the former is subject to privatization, to demands to become "more businesslike," and to cutbacks in staffing levels.

This paper does not polarize "public" and "business' administration, despite the clear motivations to do so and despite the fact that I encourage informed differentiation in all consultation.

Rather, the paper takes different conceptual ground. In outline:

- I have a characterological aversion to either/or issues.
- the realities of "public" and "private" grow more protean, and by leaps and bounds.
- *all* organizations need to distinguish between the "public interest" and a gaggle of parochial interests. Indeed, many "business" organizations (e.g., General Motors) are more vested with a public interest than many "public" agencies. Hence, some "business" targets for consultation differ radically from "public" sites, but it also seems true that differences within each of those two realms can be as great as, or greater than, the differences between them.
- *all* organizations feature a politics/administration or value/fact interface. The "line" is more or less clear, more or less permanent, and may appear at various levels, but it is always there. One learns about that "line" by getting one's ears boxed for trespassing it, whether willfully or unknowingly.
- hence the common dualities—politics versus administration, or values versus facts—do not constitute useful criteria for distinguishing between organizations even as they are clearly relevant for differentiating phenomena within any organization.
- indeed, I endorse politics *and* administration, values *and* facts, while I also caution against forgetting which is which.

Note that I do *not* propose that an "organization is an organization." Far from that, in fact. Rather, I propose a dual argument. First, my OD consultation practice emphasizes sensitivity to differences in some generic features that are applicable to all organizations. As an overlay, however, I also propose that selected features lead to especially "tough" consulting assignments and—although examples may be found in all organizations—the incidence of these selected features seems greater in some public-sector organizations. Success rates of consulting interventions do not seem to differ significantly, however.[1]

Some Generic Features in OD Consultation

There are a large number of (to me, obvious) generic features to which the observant OD consultant can refer in asymptotically describing a specific host for consultation, but I focus on only eight from that larger catalog. The purpose here is illustration, in short, not comprehensiveness.

Site Specificity

The consultant can *never* be too site-specific. This prescribes diagnosis, and then more diagnosis, whatever the broader arena in which the host exists. The variation within the public or business sector, I believe, is often as great as, and sometimes greater than, the variability between sectors. I have not reached a point where I apply a single model for diagnosis, but a range of them exist—from the usefully sparse[2] to the ponderous. I prefer to think of my mind as an inventory of such models, using several of them so as to gain multiple perspective on different facets of a host.

This may seem foolish advice in the face of today's "hoo-ha" about the simple and sovereign view that attributes *a* culture to even giant aggregations of people and resources, following the lead of Peters and Waterman's sales blockbuster *In Search of Excellence*.[3] But so much the worse for Peters and Waterman. At least since the Wehrmacht studies during World War II, to explain, the central role of "the primary group" in organizational effectiveness has been plain.[4] Some small Wehrmacht units folded in the face of combat; others fought fiercely, often onto death. Wehrmacht membership was not *the* critical variable, then. Similarly, observers[5] have long emphasized the substantial differences between the effectiveness and character of units otherwise identical in mission and role, policies, and procedures.

Recently, our research methods have caught up with the implications of such observations. The longish tradition of work with integration/differentiation,[6] for example, emphasized distinctive functional subsystems within formal systems. And more recently and explicitly, witness the efforts of those measuring organization climate or atmosphere who, following a well-accepted tradition,[7] now seek to identify distinctive subcultures, which stands in sharp contrast with overgeneralizing about a System 4 culture, or whatever, in large systems. Relatedly, our work with burnout[8] indicates that immediate workgroups—the groups of first reports—are the prime loci for burnout, not large aggregations of people. In sum, we have never found even a single smallish aggregate that did not have substantial concentrations of members in both the most- and least-advanced of eight phases.[9] Moreover, almost all immediate work groups of first reports are homogeneous with respect to the phase classifications of their members on burnout.[10]

Be site-specific, then, consultants. And it will seldom hurt to be *very* site-specific, whether the macro locus is "business" or the "public sector." Indeed, if consultants are effectively site-specific, it will matter little what the "sector" happens to be. They will have described all major relevant features of their specific host, and need not be troubled in the least with procrustean generalizations.

Presenting Symptoms-Specific

From my perspective, the effective consultant must simultaneously be a tummy-rubber and a head-patter, by which I mean to convey the sense of at once being rooted in what medical people call "presenting symptoms" but simultaneously aspiring to systemic rather than topical interventions. The presenting symptoms are often behaviors and attitudes, in brief, but the systemic view focuses not only on interaction-centered phenomena but on related structural features and associated policies and procedures.

My own specialization—Organization Development, or OD—has a checkered experience in regard to this local/systemic simultaneity. OD often has fixated on interaction-centered interventions but, as momentarily powerful as they can be, long and sometimes painful experience demonstrates that they need proximate reinforcement by structures and policies/procedures. Indeed, especially at low levels of organization and in autocratic/legalistic settings, emphasis on structure and policies/procedures *might well precede* efforts to develop appropriate interaction.[11] Details about such an approach—first structural and policy changes, even minimal ones, and only later a focus on interaction—are conveniently available.[12]

In conventional OD, oppositely, the front-load interventions tend to focus on interpersonal and group processes, progress on which provide a cultural infrastructure for the subsequent development of congenial structures and policies/procedures. First process and relationships, goes the conventional view, then task.

Value Specificity

The consultant needs to be value-specific, both in personal philosophy and in specific interventions. Oppositely, I recall with mixed feelings the local fire storm that resulted when I publicly alerted a CEO to his grievously mixed message: "They'll accept this participative stuff whether they like it or not." Whatever the arena, such value specificity seems critical to me. Indeed, the more hostile the arena, the greater the salience of values.

Now I understand this point may seem quaint, and even hopelessly naive in some consulting quarters. But my own professional value tethers—those associated with OD—are conscious and quite explicit, at least at the level of espousal.[13] I see my role as increasing the kind and amount of responsible freedom available to those in organizations, to put the matter briefly. These values serve me in direct ways. For example, as long as a consultation shows reasonable progress toward those values, I can accept even minimal interventions that approach the ideal. Specifically, our early work on flexible work hours[14] was seen as permitting some increase (albeit not magnum size) in responsible freedom in organizations, and hence we presented it as a useful design, and especially for OD openers in organizations not deemed "culturally prepared" for more intrusive interventions. Indeed, flexible work hours might even be an optimum intervention in organizations still at an autocratic stage and not yet comfortable about dealing consistently with interpersonal and group processes.

This issue has been a central one in OD consultation, in various guises. The common criticism among those giving absolute primacy to prior work on processes was direct: such efforts were incremental tinkerings at best, and cop-outs at worst. My counterreaction: You begin from where a client system, is in general, rather than from where you might like it to be.

Hierarchy- and Function-Specific

In addition, I propose, the consultant needs to be hierarchically and functionally specific always and ever. This specificity will provide far more directly interpretable data than information about which sector a consultant happens to be operating in.

The underlying proposition needs little elaboration: where one sits often influences what one sees, as well as how one feels and behaves. Lawrence and Lorsch's work,[15] for example, points to the several significant various differences that a consultant might well expect between R & D and manufacturing, even in the same organization—in time horizons and felt pressures, and so on.

Stage- or Phase-Specific

Even simplistic notions help in getting the consultant to follow this advice: Not only begin from where your client happens to be, but intervene in such ways as to ease the movement toward where the client will soon go. Thus General Motors might be located along this developmental path: beginning with an entrepreneurial rush, plateauing as a cumbersome bureaucracy in the 1960s and 1970s, and struggling in the 1980s to become effectively postbureaucratic.[16] Reasonable consultant interventions at one of those gross stages or phases could well be poison at one or another of the others. Worse still, a consultant intervention that helped a client at the bureaucratic stage might make more difficult the subsequent transition to a postbureaucratic condition, absent a tempering of the then present by the soon to be present.

The point is often encountered at micro levels. Consultants might well distinguish two major phases or stages of small-group life: when the prime focus is on allocating power if influence, and when that focus is on personalness or affect.[17] The same behavior—e.g., patting someone on the head—might be interpreted in radically different ways in those two phases, as condescending in the former case or as affectionate in the latter. The phase-specific consultant will make the appropriate interpretation in planning a useful intervention.

Aware consultants also can put phase specificity to good use at macro levels. Consider these familiar stages for growth:[18]

- add to volume at central site
- add field units
- add functions or activities
- diversify product lines

These phases often are experienced progressively, but two or more basic growth strategies might overlap, consciously or by inadvertence.

Appropriate consultant interventions need to be informed about such phases, or mixes of them. Prescribing a good dose of the bureaucratic principles would be reasonable for the first strategy, but it can cause increasing mischief for the two following stages. That conventional advice would be seriously counterproductive for diversification, whether in place or in immediate prospect.

Not so incidentally, efforts to reform public management might have been well served by an awareness of such phases. Early encouragement[19] for public-sector applications of structural innovations that decades earlier appeared in business settings—e.g., the range from divisionalization and the matrix through job enrichment—tended to fall on deaf ears. In part, this was due to the fact that those innovations were long-delayed responses to earlier and often painful efforts at diversification in some businesses.[20] But diversification—except perhaps in Defense—was not much characteristic of federal public agencies until the late 1960s and 1970s. Consider the Forest Service, which had developed a towering reputation for the effective and honest monomanagement of trees, to exagerrate a bit but not very much. The diversification of the late 1960s and beyond proved a tough nut, in part because the earlier specialization constituted a substantial learned incapacity when it came to dealing with hordes of multiple users—e.g., hunters and tourists, especially, as well as sylvan scientists—and even more so when it came to dealing with Job Corps training and the urban backgrounds of most trainees.

Somewhat the same point might apply with equal force to otherwise well-intentioned efforts to extend "North American" managerial and organization development to Third-World settings.[21] Note the common aversion to "spoils politics" in development prescriptions, as if Western experts wished that overseas clients would avoid an often painful part of their history. Note an unexpected consequence, however. "Spoils politics" was central in the growth of Western-style political parties, and "skipping that part" might well have serious—even profound—consequences for political development in the myopic pursuit of technocratic quick fixes.

Demography-Specific

The aware consultant needs to be demography-specific, in addition. In very real senses, that is to say, our destiny is implied by demographics. Hence effective consulting interventions need to be mindful of extant and probable demographics.

I recall a personal experience, even a jolting "aha"! I was engaged as a consultant by the Tennessee Valley Authority (TVA) in the early 1970s. The picture in my mind was the TVA of the 1935–50 era: aggressive in its social mission of bringing power to the impoverished countryside, providing a "yardstick" against which to measure the rates of private generators of electricity, and so on. I met the entire managerial staff in a large auditorium. What I saw were grey heads, many bald, and almost all male; and what I learned soon was that most of them were far more interested in maintenance than in change or renewal, and reasonably so. I took an informal poll, and learned that my audience clustered in the 60 to 62 age interval!

I became demography-specific in a hurry. Not surprisingly—given a little reflection that should have been anticipation—I could explain the discrepancy between my head and my eyes. Many idealistic youngsters joined TVA at its birth, in 1935. They tended to stay—basically for love of the region, and because many got early promotions in the early elaboration of the Authority. These attractions had negative consequences. To oversimplify, young recruits—and especially those representing new disciplines or professions like atomic energy or representing changed social conditions for Blacks and women—these young recruits were few and far between. Low turnover exacerbated the effects of tailing-off growth. Hence, agency personnel—and especially management—were chronologically a lot older in 1970+, and their common maturing impacted the Authority.

The point is not idiosyncratic. Pfeffer[22] generalizes usefully about demography as destiny, for example. And employees of most universities or colleges will soon enough recognize the basic point in very direct and sometimes painful ways. American colleges boomed in the 1965–75 interval, and they perforce hired major proportions of their professional cadres from a narrow cluster of ages. Faculties began aging and tenuring, in an age-specific clump, with consequences that are yet to exert their full impacts. For example, two effects—the peaking of college enrollments in the late 1970s and early 1980s, and the general raising of the retirement age from 65 to 70—left few spaces for new and younger recruits. Tenure policies will create more intense issues in academia than exist in many other arenas, and perhaps especially because many of the unfulfilled and frustrated would-be recruits are technically far better prepared than their seniors. With the bulk of many faculties now in their late 40s or early 50s, another effect is also clear. Fifteen or twenty years from how—absent concerted early retirement programs—higher education will be hit with a tsunami of personnel changes. Pessimists also might predict heightened attack and defense as this peak period approaches.

Context- or Immediate Environment-Specific

The useful consultant needs to position interventions so that they are context-specific, or responsive to the client's immediate environment. The point is obvious, and yet is often neglected. I have in mind the consultant hired to work on an overseas "morale problem" affecting Americans and locals. Industrious efforts at a quick fix by means of team-building resulted mostly in educating the consultant that the source of the "morale problem" was less tractable than interaction or relationships—the grossly higher salaries and fringes paid to Americans, for the same quality of effort on the same or similar jobs.

This prescription will become manifest in such numerous ways that only bare illustration is possible here. Consider two organizations—one in ethical pharmaceuticals and the other in bulk chemicals. Both are "business" organizations, but that incidental pales in comparison to the differences in their contexts or immediate environments. These differences have manifold causes/consequences, at least some of them being accidentals such as that chemicals had not yet experienced their equivalent of Senator Estes Kefauver and his well-publicized investigations of the pharmaceutical industry. At least to this point, Bhopal and the numerous Love Canals seem not to have done to—and for—the chemical industry what Kefauver and crew did to/for pharmaceuticals. Other differences inhere in the nature of the broad politicoeconomic-technical arenas which the firms reside—e.g., the size of profit margins and the consequent attention that will be given to pollution, broadly defined, to the quality of working life, and to the character and quality of labor/management relations, among many other factors.

Whatever the sources/consequences of such contextual differences, the bottom line for present purposes has a bold and simple character. A reasonable consultant intervention in one context might well be perceived as uninformed, insensitive, counterproductive, or even grossly illegal in the other.

Similarly, compare two Georgia public agencies, both in transportation. They differ profoundly, nonetheless, as is reflected in one overall assessment: "We in the state's Department of Transportation are in much the same business as MARTA, or the Metropolitan Atlanta Rapid Transit Authority; and we could do what they're doing. But their 10-year program would take us about 50 years."

Briefly, the two agencies operate in different contexts. Thus one agency is enmeshed in state politics, and has been for a long time, while the other has a specific and local character; and MARTA was deliberately set up not to be "just another government agency," with various flexibilities as to compensation, etc., intended to encourage quicker reaction times.

In today's diversified organizations, signally, local contexts or immediate environments often are on collision courses. Patently, Sales often will see a world different from that of Manufacturing, establishing again that few of us consistently or for very long transcend our context or immediate environment, without signal effort. The present point applies in other senses as well. For example, I recall one of the fiercest and least-redemptive conflicts to which I was a party as consultant. *The* issue was the degree of cleanliness of a plant's floors, a situation barely saved from the bizarre category by some elemental contextual dynamics. The plant's management "team" had similar personal profiles: upwardly mobile, ambitious, and aggressive, working for the next job or two by means of brief rotations through a soap plant. Although all worked for the same corporation, about half of the "team" had an industrial orientation and the other half had strong consumer-products backgrounds, especially in cake mixes! The concern "about cleanliness" had contextual as well as personal roots, in short.

Some readers may sense a "whoops" here. In urging recognition of and response to contexts or immediate environments I may be allowing a back-door entrance of the public versus business distinction. Well, yes but mostly no. To the degree that the focus of a constultant's work in a public agency is affected by broad constraints—civil service regulations, legislative mandates, and so on—I clearly here urge awareness of and response to that context. Elsewhere,[23] indeed, I detail some consultative challenges I have encountered with an unusual frequency in public-sector consultation. A few of those higher-frequency examples are cited in the last section of this paper. My present point is at once more general and robust. Detailed diagnosis is necessary in all cases, and the consultant must attend to more finely-tuned discriminations than public versus business in responding to differences in context or immediate environment.

Cultures-Specific

The aware consultant must be cultures-specific, and the plural is used advisedly. The present point applies in at least three senses.

The consultant is *always* in multiple cultures, and should be, to begin. Thus many clients—even smallish units of firms or agencies—can have distinctive cultures. For example, one of my clients has such a preoccupation with ties as part of their formal dress code that we—quite solemnly—negotiated a contractual provision providing a daily fee for my "*appropriately* wearing a *suit-*

able tie'' (my emphases). (I believe the ''appropriately'' and ''suitable'' reflect not distrust but rather client's concern about my possible insouciance, as in sporting a Donald Duck tie in my breast pocket!). Another client proscribes short-sleeved dress shirts, tie or no. In such small matters, and larger ones as well, lack of culture-specific sensitivity can damage an otherwise mutually profitable relationship.

The point is not a subtle one, but I encourage consultants to go through an explicit ''culture audit.'' You can learn some useful things, and early in the game. See Table 12.1. My ''culture audit'' turned up this bit of possibly important information, even though I smoke only an occasional cigar.

Table 12.1

Item:	One client's offices showed no smoking or smokers.
Learning:	Not surprisingly, it soon became clear that the CEO held a strong opinion in this matter.
Reality test:	Many people did smoke, and often at work.
Critical indicator:	An absolute sign of trust and acceptance was sharing knowledge about ''safe zones'' and smoking at work in your presence.
Questions for the future:	How many other mock observances existed? Was the CEO out of touch, or was the reality of issues less important than appearances?

Moreover, the effective consultant is a ''marginal person,'' by definition, marginal in the sense of having a base in numerous cultures. Thus one's professional code of ethics, or one's firm, or whatever, provides a more or less permanent membership. And one's client provides another, and potentially very different, set of social systems. The consultant who ''goes native'' often will suffer a reduced capacity to help, but the consultant as ''alien'' typically will have little or no occasion to be effective. Here consultants need to be cultures-specific, with all the potential for cross-pressures implied in that usage.

Finally, on this eighth perspective on specificity, sensitivity to various macro cultures is increasingly useful, and often necessary. Whether the contact involves women, gays, blacks, Japanese trading partners, or whomever, the issue of broad cultural specificity can have a substantial salience. The folk lore is full of mutual misperceptions, gaffes, or worse.

Some Probabilistic Differences, Perhaps

Let me now isolate a class of features that might well have a somewhat greater incidence in public-sector consultation, despite their occurrence elsewhere. The list here is highly selective and sketchy, but both a longer list and greater details are conveniently available.[24] Four points get attention, and the consultant might put them on a priority list for early checking when working in the public sector, especially at the upper levels.

"Slough of Despond, Pall of Fear"

In my experience, public-sector consultation is more likely than business to contain cases with dominant and difficult features. Elsewhere, and perhaps too fancifully, I refer to these features as the "slough of despond and the pall of fear."[25] Such effects derive from multiple factors, including contemporary bureaucracy bashing but perhaps more centrally—especially at the federal level—due to a simultaneous plateau in federal employment and a precipitous increase in senior civil servants opting for (or even coerced into) retirement in the last 10 to 15 years.

Whatever the contributors, the condition (when it exists) poses severe challenges for the consultant, whether in government or in business. For OD intervenors, for example, the derivative focus is far less on public confrontation and far more on the various forms of collective empowerment and of inducing strength through mutual agreements. These can be approached by charting areas of "wriggle room," and especially by facing the key question: "What is the worst thing that can happen if . . . ?"

Crisis of Agreement

Perhaps relatedly, my public-sector experience seems to contain a higher percentage of cases of "crisis of agreement," of "going to Abilene." Some such notion can be traced most directly to Janis' "groupthink,"[26] and its fetching restatement in both folksy and analytic terms is due to Jerry Harvey—alone[27] and with Albertson.[28]

Basically, the vicious dynamics of a "conflict of agreement" inhere in one of two basic conditions: a strong pull ("We're great people in a great group"); or a feared push ("I'm not that good, I know, and I'll do anything to maintain membership because I can never duplicate what I have here"). In both cases, loss of membership is consequential. Hence people may not talk to one another about commonly perceived problems or solutions to them, even when they happen to share problems/solutions. The paradox is that this actual agreement goes unspoken, often because each individual fears being the only sheep among goats, and hence chooses silence rather than risking membership or status.

"Crisis of agreement" seems far more difficult a target for helpful consultant interventions than does disagreement or conflict. Reasonable guidelines have been developed,[29] but only anecdotal evidence exists concerning the design's appropriateness. My up-front habit involves a resort to honesty. I advise clients, on diagnosing a conflict of agreement, that the process will be long and arduous, with success rates being uncertain. Absent a conflict of agreement, I am ebullient with regard to my standard team-building design: Certain predicted changes will occur in three of every four cases, on average, or there is no fee!

Complicating Power/Status Dynamics

In my experience, power/status dynamics involving the consultant's role seem more common and virulent in the public sector. In one interpretation, a loosely coupled system may be said to be particularly vulnerable to having its delicate equilibrium threatened by any new participant, and all the more so by a consultant who may be specially credentialed and highly paid.

Consultants must find their own way in how to be impactful while avoiding being seen merely as just another competitor for power/status. I find that idealistic protestations of being only a "helper" or "facilitator" do not much impress those concerned acutely about power/status, although my experience may be atypical. Rather, declarations of self-interest seem to go down better. Hence I have said:

> Why am I here? Well, the money's welcome, but my dominant commitment is to get publishable results. Typically, that means a successful intervention. Moreover, I am not overly fond of failure. Although one can learn from failure, I prefer success. So I succeed when you and the agency progress.

Hence, even my most deliberate "helping" or "facilitating" seem to be accepted better in the context of explicit self-interest. Perhaps that is because the position in fact approaches the truth, at least sufficiently and often enough.

Consultant as "Silent Servant"

In my experience, finally, public-sector consultation more often has a "silent servant" quality than do business arenas. I do not mean this happens always or often in the public arena; but it happens to me almost not at all in business consultation. What is "silent servant" expected to do? Well, you know the old joke: "A consultant is a person who steals your watch, and then tells you the time." "Silent servant" consultants have a different role, and fate: They are "told" by the client, subtly or boldly—not only that there is *a* watch but what time it shows; and consultants are employed on the high probability that they will faithfully report to others about *that* watch and *that* time.

I may seem cavalier in this regard, but I zealously try to avoid the "silent servant" role. Certainly it is easier for me to "be principled" in this regard, being well-supported in my university role. So I may appear as a radical in this matter, but one with his rent paid, victuals supplied, and personal computer maintained. If that is the appearance, so be it.

My public view, at least, is that "silent servant" helps neither client nor consultant. And I care enough for both to try to avoid demeaning either, given that even the most vigilant can be fooled on occasion.

*Paper prepared for delivery at the 50th Annual Meeting, Academy of Management, Chicago, Ill., August 11–13, 1986.

Notes

1. Robert T. Golembiewski, Carl W. Proehl, Jr., and David Sink, "Estimating the Success of OD Applications," *Training and Development Journal* 72 (1982): 86–95.
2. M. Weisbord, "Orgainzation Dynamics," *Group and Organization Studies* 1 (1976): 430–47.
3. Thomas J. Peters and Robert H. Waterman, Jr. *In Search of Excellence* (New York: Harper & Row (1982).
4. E. A. Shils and M. Horowitz, "Cohesion and Disintegration in the Wehrmacht in World War II," *Public Opinion Quarterly* 12 (1948): 281–315.
5. E.g., J. D. Thompson, "Authority and Power in Two 'Identical' Organizations," *American Journal of Sociology* 62 (1956): 290–301; and C. T. Goodsell, *The Case for Bureaucracy* (Chatham, N.J.: Chatham House 1985), 30–55.
6. P. R. Lawrence, and J. W. Lorsch. *Organization and Environment* (Homewood, Ill.: Irwin 1969).
7. *Ibid.*
8. R. T. Golembiewski, R. Munzenrider, and J. Stevenson. *Stress in Organizations* (New York: Praeger (1986), 180–94.
9. R. T. Golembiewski, et al., "The Epidemiology of Progressive Phases of Burnout," *Journal of Health and Human Resources Administration* (1986), in press.
10. E.g., B. Rountree, "Psychological Burnout in Task Groups," *Journal of Health and Human Resources Administration* 7 (1984): 235–48.
11. For an overview, see Robert T. Golembiewski, *Approaches to Planned Change*. New York: Marcel Dekker (1979), vols. I and II.
12. E.g., Robert T. Golembiewski. *Humanizing Public Organizations*. Mt. Airy, Md.: Lomond Publications (1985).
13. E.g., Golembiewski, *Approaches to Planned Change*, vol. I, chaps. 1–4.
14. Robert T. Golembiewski, Richard Hilles, and Munro Kagno, "A Longitudinal Study of Flexi-Time Effects," *Journal of Applied Behavioral Science* 10 (Dec. 1979): 503–32.
15. Lawrence and Lorsch, *Organization and Environment*.
16. P. M. Carrigan, "Up from the Ashes," *OD Practitioner* 18 (1986): 1–6.
17. W. G. Bennis and H. A. Shepard, "A Theory of Group Development," *Human Relations* 9 (1956): 415–37.
18. A. D. Chandler, Jr. *Strategy and Structure*. Cambridge, Mass.: M.I.T. Press (1962).

19. Robert T. Golembiewski, "Civil Service and Managing Work," *American Political Science Review* 56 (1962): 961–73.
20. Chandler, *Strategy and Structure*.
21. K. L. Murrell, "Africa and Organization Development," *Organization Development Journal* 4 (1986): 53–60.
22. J. Pfeffer. *Organizations* (Marshfield, Mass.: Pitman 1982): 277–93.
23. Golembiewski, *Humanizing Public Organization*.
24. *Ibid*.
25. *Ibid.*, 235–45.
26. I. Janis, *Groupthink* (Boston: Houghton Mifflin 1972).
27. J. B. Harvey, "The Abilene Paradox," *Organizational Dynamics* 7 (1974): 63–80.
28. J. B. Harvey and D. R. Albertson, "Neurotic Organizations," Parts I and II. *Personnel Journal* 50 (1971): 694–99 and 770–77.
29. See the summary in Golembiewski, *Approaches to Planned Change*, vol. II, 152–61.

13

Is OD Narrowly Culture-Bound? Well, Yes; and Then, No

This editorial takes on the general character of Martin Buber's genial response to *the* central question: Is humankind good or bad?

Buber is said to have replied: "Yes."

I am of a similar mind when it comes to one of the central contemporary issues about OD. Is OD narrowly culture-bound, or is it in some senses universalistic?

Let my answer be direct: Yes.

This response is neither precious nor diplomatic. For the question is serious, and so is the answer. Moreover, since taking sides on the question is both frequent and spirited,[1] fence-sitting is likely to attract attention if not derision from the committed in both camps. And the "Yes" answer may seem to avoid an answer, rather than to provide one.

The case for OD's cultureboundedness is both clear and long standing. After all, OD burst into prominence at a particular place (in North America, or certainly in "the West"), at a specific time (roughly the post–World War II period), in response to the demands of relatively advanced technology (refineries loom large in OD's early history), and in societies with quite prominent and even novel features—those coping with greater mobility and higher levels of education and training, for example, and in societies also trying to contain insistent demands for shares in the new affluence coming from a growing chorus of newly vocal and more numerous claimants. Moreover, OD has definite orientations to cultural artifacts: the early interaction-centered OD designs presumed at least a moderate or even small social distance, if not a T-Group kind of socioemotional closeness; and OD philosophy contained liberal dollops of emphases considered strange if not seditious in some settings, as in biases toward greater power equalization, or even in pronouncements that "mutual empowerment is a mutual good."

Indeed, even the fundaments of OD have implied its culturally loaded character. Recall the time-honored advice to "begin from where the client is," which assumes that OD's goal of a "new culture at work" often will stand in sharp contrast with typical cultures at work.

So who can question the strong case that can be made for OD as culture-bound? Not many did. Or do.

Hence it was that much useful work sought what might be called "good fits" between OD designs and specific cultural features. For example, the work of Hofstede[2] got much attention. Although the bloom is most definitely off the details of that particular rose, the basic notion still has a great deal of currency. How can certain interaction-centered designs "work" under conditions of a "culture of silence," for example, which we are told by people who know exists in many Third-World settings? And how could various "high touch" designs be applicable when prevailing cultural norms often seem to sanction nonconfrontation and avoidance, especially of powerful or respected personages?

Jaeger recently[3] has done us the substantial favor of detailing a number of such "good fit" or "bad fit" combinations of cultural features and OD designs. He builds on the earlier and similar effort by Hofstede himself.[4] For example, Jaeger sees sharp limits on the use of sensitivity training or directly confrontive designs in traditional autocratic or paternalistic societies, among which he numbers most or all of South America. And Jaeger sees survey/feedback as widely applicable, because it can generate useful information in all settings while permitting anonymity and moderating the direct confrontation of authorities.

So I repeat myself: Who can question the strong case for OD as culture-bound?

Well, not that it proves anything in particular, but I have begun to question that case in several senses. Let me share four of the more direct components of my recent questioning, which was accentuated by surveys about success rates of OD applications in various settings. As I say, I started that study, and now it has an intellectual half nelson on my attention. Two selections in Part II sketch some of the results of this recent preoccupation of mine, but on to four immediate points about culture boundedness.

First, it just might be that highly variable cultural features coexist with relatively homogeneous personal features. In earlier days, from this point of view, many would have juxtaposed several "national characters" with a "human nature." The "characters" are real and powerful, each constituting a "nurture" that develops idiosyncratically for very complicated historical reasons—as is allegedly the case with the court Spanish of an earlier day, which I am told was spoken with a lisp because (how could it be otherwise?) the king was so afflicted. In this view, also, "human nature" constitutes a kind of common underlying stratum on top of which all manner of cultural artifacts have been built.

Some consider this "human nature" to be a result of a divine spirit in which all people share. Other variants propose some common set of needs that all or almost all people will seek to fulfill, at least when it is safe to try.

This generic "nature" will be variously constrained by one or another specific "nurture," but on occasions—sometimes rare, sometimes frequent—the "nature" will assert itself. Moreover, that "nature" is always a threat to assert itself, with a long-term inability to do so being expressed in dissatisfaction and frustration. The sense of it suggests the tectonic plates resting on the earth's magma. At times, all seems very calm, but this only masks the continuous massive geologic forces at work underneath. At other times, those forces become manifest, making it plain what is always churning beneath the surface.

Now, I'm not sure I want to buy-in to a full-blown sense of "human nature," but I do see a lot of OD designs touching something at the core of most people with whom I work. More and more, these people come from all quarters and all cultures, from representative political contexts as well as from autocratic and even tyrannical ones. And almost all people prefer to be open and owning, and experience a strong sense of relief and well-being when they are. Similarly, almost all luxuriate in a task over which they can exert control and for which they can be responsible. This seems to me evidence that people relish being encouraged, or even permitted, to express their central or essential qualities, to meet their "deeper needs." In this sense, "nature" asserts itself when it has a reasonable chance.

This does not mean that most of us, most of the time, act consonantly with this "nature." But most people seem to know when they violate it, and they regret doing so. I have dealt with some rough characters, and some of their behaviors can credibly be labeled brutal. But even these characters tend to note that—with sincerity, I believe—"It's a shame it can't be a different world."

To the degree that OD variously touches such centralities or essentialities, of course, so does OD qualify as more univeralistic than as narrowly culture-bound.

Second, even if the "good fit" case is watertight, it does not follow that only culturally congruent OD designs are the best, or even tolerable. This is the case in two senses. Thus a people may need what their culture does *not* favor, or even directly proscribes. In the extreme case, the survival of a culture may require precisely what that culture rejects, either implicitly or explicitly.

This constitutes no call to go around, willy-nilly, imposing OD's brand of salvation on the masses, yearning to be authentic. Rather, the focus is on how appropriate action-research designs can help raise appropriate consciousness, and then to help useful things to happen even in cultures that have been marching to other drums for very long periods.

How can this be done? Consider an action research application to "river blindness" among impoverished villagers, some of whom had recently gained literacy. The design has these basic elements:[5]

- The village elders were approached as to whether it would be appropriate to train the newly literate in learning about river blindness—with the possibility of doing some remedial work, *if* the need were established, and *if* the elders and villagers agreed to the program for intervention.
- A survey of river blindness was conducted by the newly literate as part of their training—identifying the incidence and distribution of symptoms, which were widespread.
- Elders and villagers authorized another step.
- Local knowledge about river blindness was revealed in dialog with the villagers and, as appropriate, new knowledge/skills were melded with the local knowledge.
- The newly literate designed and began an ameliorative program.
- The newly literate evaluated the intervention, and reported to the elders and other villagers.

If the elders had not consented, or if things had come undone somewhere else along the way, that would have required going back to the drawing board. It has *always* been this way in OD, which prescribes going to the pain or the problem as a stimulus for action. No pain, no gain.

So the military often requires: Hurry up, and wait.

OD urges: Wait, and then hurry!

Third, some OD designs seem to have a broad spectrum of applicability. Jaeger makes that point about survey or feedback designs,[6] for example, which are intentionally tailored to the host's culture. This characterization not only applies to a well-designed survey, which should blend boilerplate items with those steeped in the local culture—in topic, relevance, *and* perhaps especially in phrasing.[7] Moreover, cultural nuances are taken into account by means of the action-planning groups that are part of any well-run survey/feedback intervention.

Not surprisingly, at least on reflection, various interaction-centered designs also seem to have a broad-spectrum applicability. Third-party conflict resolution efforts may apply in many cultural settings. Their privatizing character encourages their applicability of social distance in both high and low settings, for example. Various process-oriented interventions, including T-Group variants, also have been widely used, and with reported success. In such designs, cultural nuances are the central targets of process analysis. Hence the cultural sensitivity of such designs is high, given responsive facilitators and persistent participants.

In sum, this third point suggests that OD designs are far from peas in a pod when it comes to their degree of cultural boundedness.

Fourth, as noted in the preceding editorial, the full range of OD designs has in fact been applied to a broad range of cultural settings. Estimates of success rates appear to be somewhat lower in nonaffluent than in conventional settings, but they are still substantial. This final point suggests in a global sense that the corpus of OD designs are culturally specific in only attenuated senses that need quite precise specification.

So let us return for a third time to the focal issue: Who can question the strong case that can be made for OD as narrowly culture-bound?

The four robust points just introduced provide some sense of why this writer has come to just such a questioning posture about what has been a part of our common wisdom.

Notes

1. See the exchange between Marshall Sashkin and Edgar Schein in the Academy of Management, *OD Newsletter*, Winter 1986, 4–7.
2. Geert Hofstede, *Culture's Consequences* (Reading, Mass.: Addison-Wesley, 1980).
3. Alfred M. Jaeger, "The Appropriateness of Organization Development Outside North America," *International Studies of Man and Organization* 14 (1984): 23–35. See also his "Organization Development and National Culture," *Academy of Management Review* 11 (No. 1, 1986): 178–90.
4. Geert Hofstede, "Motivation, Leadership, and Organization," *Organizational Dynamics* 9 (Summer 1980): 42–63.
5. G. Belloncle, "Toward a New Method in Rural Development in West Africa," *Rural Africana* 10 (Winter: 1981), 1–7.
6. Jaeger, "The Appropriateness of Organization Development outside North America."
7. For details about some of the tricks of the surveyer's trade, see Robert T. Golembiewski and Richard Hilles, *Toward the Responsive Organization* (Salt Lake City: Brighton Publishing, 1979).

Part II

WHAT OD MIGHT BECOME

Part IV

WHAT OR MIGHT BECOME

Introduction

Twelve thought pieces comprise this second part of *Ideas and Issues*, focusing on the general theme—What OD Might Become. Conveniently, the essays may be viewed as representing three kinds of action:

- realistic and responsible *horn-blowing* about OD's success rates (selections 14 through 18);
- significant *tethering* of the OD field and its practitioners (selections 19 through 21); and
- aspects of *visioning* about OD's future (selections 22 through 25)

Brief comments will introduce each of these twelve selections, with the goal of providing the reader with a kind of rough map to a complicated and even rugged terrain.

1. OD and realistic horn blowing: selections 14 through 18. The five initial pieces relate to aspects of how well OD goes about its business. Two questions get dominant attention, in effect. What are reasonable estimates of OD success rates? And how do OD practitioners present the good news, or the bad news, about success rates? The second question comes complete with some speculations as to why OD practitioners deal as curiously as they do with success rates.

"So, What About Success Rates?" gets us off to a direct start. The general OD mode with respect to OD efficacy is a very restrained enthusiasm, at best. This is curious, given that numerous available evaluative studies all but unanimously indicate substantial success rates, even formidable ones. This underenthusiasm, even pessimism, might have been more appropriate in the early days—the 1960s and 1970s—when few evaluative studies existed, and when even those rarities dealt with small panels of applications, almost all in North American settings. More recently, the number of such studies has increased sharply, and one of them reviews over 500 OD applications. Moreover, overseas applications are no longer rare.

Two relative constants remain. Thus success rates do not require apology. Moreover, the basic underwhelming approach to success rates has not changed, in effect. However, silence[1] has now largely replaced most of the earlier pessimistic handwringing.

To be sure, most of these estimates might overestimate "success," since they basically involve Western and often high-technology settings. "An Even Better Kept Secret: Success Rates in Third-World Applications" dwells on the results of a test of this significant point. Sure enough, the estimated success rate is lower than for panels largely representing the "developed nations." But that success rate is still substantial, especially given the nature of the problems dealt with and the resource-poor character of Third World settings.

Yet a third kind of test of success rates is referred to in "We Are Not Here to Reinvent the Status Quo." A search was made for OD applications in economically disadvantaged settings in countries with a high GNP per capita, so as to permit a test of the common charge that OD designs usually involve affluents and hence would be substantially inapplicable in resource-poor settings. Few such cases exist, but they have a success rate that does not discourage more expansive applications under economic deprivation.

So the evaluative studies seem to generate substantial success rates, on balance, even under trying conditions. So why the underwhelming response of most OD practitioners?

"You Can't Be A Beacon . . . ," I and II, try to provide some perspective on this curiosity. Most ODers—or at least those who write for publication—cannot be accused of overselling success rates, and this point gets scrutiny from a number of angles. For example, one explanation of the silence about success rates proposes that it is due to a concern about the inadequate methodology underlying available evaluation studies. That is a perfectly defensible position, of course: one would be foolish to emphasize attractive success rates while suspecting the methods used to estimate them. But silence? The basic issue here is that ODers preach greater openness and owning, in general, so any explanation emphasizing silence about inadequate methodology requires an assumption that ODers are false to their own espoused theory.

The two pieces of "Beacon . . ." detail a number of other possible interpretations of the underwhelming reaction to the results of evaluations of OD applications. They reach no definite conclusion, and in that sense the basic issue becomes more and more curious. But those two selections do raise many possibilities, and consider their character and probable impact.

2. OD and required tethering: selections 19 through 21. The five preceding selections suggest that the technology-cum-values called Organization Development, or OD, has substantial power. Because of that fact, the issue of how OD might be appropriately tethered assumes major proportions. Otherwise, OD might well become an unguided missile, powerful but poorly aimed.

Three selections below address aspects of this tethering—first from the perspective of the field of OD, and then from the perspective of the individual

OD consultant. Various selections in the other two parts of this book also relate to this crucial tethering. For example, Part I includes such relevant selections as: "Why OD?: Putting Values in Their Prominent Place" and "OD as
Increasing Responsible Freedom in Organizations." In addition, Part III provides these relevant selections, among others: " 'A Statement of Values and
Ethics . . . ,' " and "ODers as Servants of Power: Temptations and Countertendencies."

At the macro level, OD has to be concerned about both its conceptual
roommates and landlords, as it were, an issue which in practice has grown in
salience as OD's reputation has burgeoned. Is OD just Human Resource Management? That represents one common version of who or what tethers whom.
I answer this question in the negative, especially because of the values underlying OD and even though OD commonly resides in an HR department.

One selection below deals with a more tricky example of the general
issue—"Is QWL OD's Charge? Or Vice Versa?: Why It Matters Who Gets
Custody." QWL refers to Quality of Working Life, of course, and it still constitutes the basic identification of many organizational change agents even
though some observers see decreasing reliance on that label.[2] Basically, the
essay proposes that OD should get custody of QWL, as it were, on the basic
grounds that OD values and process analysis provide necessary and prior constraints on QWL, whose ranks include many of those with useful job design
and systems-analytic skills. Absent guidance by the OD focus on interaction
and human relationships, to put the point another way, QWL might be inclined to focus on narrow efficiency as the goal for directing and judging attempts to design jobs and systems.

Two subsequent selections provide microperspective on the issue of tethering OD. Both focus on a fateful choice—the conditions under which one
should provide consultation services, or withhold them. Put another way, the
first rule of OD consultancy may well be: Find a client. But that good advice
needs multiple specification—which kind of client, for how long, and under
what circumstances?

"Judas Goats and Providing or Withholding Consultation," to introduce
the first of this pair, uses a perhaps strange metaphor to draw attention to an
old point. "Judas goats" are animal stooges used in slaughterhouses to lead
cattle to their fate, for which service the Judas goat is allowed to live and even
prosper. The essay distinguishes four varieties of the species, so as to warn
OD consultants of the several ways in which the unwary can fall into an awkward habit.

"Value Complementarity and Providing or Withholding Consultation"
raises a related issue, but a more complex and confounding one. The basic
question is direct: What degree of congruence between the values of a client
and an OD consultant is sufficient to justify the provision of services? The

difficulties and even dilemmas raised by this question severely challenge thought and practice.

"Value complementarity" is easier to describe than resolve, then, and bare illustration constitutes the present goal. Spotlighting some central issues here relies on a basic contrast: between the comprehensive approach to OD efforts, and one labeled "limited social contract." The first often uses a "seeding" approach to OD, which eventually generates not only a "critical mass" of advocates of choice and change, but also a work culture or climate of regenerative interaction that will induce the development of appropriately reinforcing structures, policies, and procedures in an organization. In opposition, OD as limited social contract isolates manageable targets for realistic "next bites" for moving incrementally toward a more responsibly free organization. These two contributors to a basic contrast do not exhaust the possibilities, but they do serve to suggest the costs/benefits of two common venues for OD applications.

3. OD and visioning: selections 22 through 25. What OD might become both builds upon, and is restricted by, what we envision for it—by what we dream, by what we see as ideal, as conditioned by some complex appreciation of what is "do-able." Four selections below carry the present burden of some limited visioning for OD.

"Toward Enhancing OD's Future" presents overall perspective on what needs to be done in order to raise the probability of a viable tomorrow. Five emphases dominate, and they all take this common form: OD will have a viable institutional future to the degree that it. . . .

The prognoses in that essay also take the same form. Failure to accomplish those five emphases in sufficient degree not only will negate OD's future, *but should do so*. If OD cannot do the required job, it not only will step aside but should be pushed away.

A second selection has both a long title and a difficult task—"Toward a Contingency View of Certification: Professionalization, Performance, and Protectionism." Over the years, in sum, the ante has been raised concerning what constitutes caring and competent OD practice. This raising of the ante has become manifest in many ways, one of which is by way of greater trappings of professionalization that may eventuate in the certification of practitioners. The issue has been with ODers for more than a decade, and it comes and goes in its severity as a factor that elevates blood pressures.

This second selection under the visioning theme seeks to sketch the major trade-offs involved in the three Ps—Professionalization, Performance, and Protectionism. That is, to provide the short form of the argument, some see greater professionalization as tied quite directly to enhanced performance, while others see the consequences of professionalization as more likely to produce protectionism and stultification. In effect, the three Ps circumscribe the basic battleground within which protagonist and antagonist strut their stuff on the subject of the certification of ODers.

Developing contingency views may be stimulating, even fun, but they can never replace choice making. "Toward OD Certification: 'It's Not My Dog, Mister,' " sketches my personal position on certification. Basically, the selection proposes getting on with it, but in ways that progressively build on the sense of community among ODers. So it will not be certification tomorrow, for that would be premature. But neither can one simply deny responsibility for what other self-professed ODers do, for that is dangerous and ultimately self-defeating.

The penultimate—some might say presumptuous—expression of the third theme is found in the last selection in this second part of *Ideas and Issues*. "Toward A National Institute of Planned and Peaceful Change: Visioning about Our Future"—there, that says it all.

This final visioning selection proposes a three-facet model for structuring a macro expression of what OD might become. These facts deal with: the several classes of appropriate OD designs; the several levels at which they can be applied, from the individual through various international systems; and the time frame of the intervention, from emergency reaction to long-range prevention. These facets clearly constitute only a point of departure, but even such talking points can be useful in providing a sense of what OD might move toward and of the institutional form in which its values and technology might find a suitable home.

Notes

1. For an exception, see Michael Beer and Anna Elise Walton, "Organization Development and Change," *Annual Review of Psychology* 38 (1987): 341–43.
2. Beer and Walton, 354.

14

"So, What about Success Rates?"

Not very long ago, OD circles were awash in pained and pessimistic pronouncements. One could not go to a meeting of the OD Network or the Academy of Management without being engulfed in assessments that emphasized OD's multiple awkwardness—OD as adolescent, in the throes of an identity crisis, as having severe growing pains, as paying too little attention to its failures, as applicable only with great difficulty in large bureaucracies, and so on through a very long and dreary catalog.

Published messages were even more somber, in the aggregate. Virtually any issue of the *Journal of Applied Behavioral Science* or similar trade publications also was chockablock with similar alarum. Most common in such loci was the concern that OD "is not rigorous," with the usual criteria being loosely derived from a natural science context and emphasizing "experimental" modes of inquiry appropriate for the formulation of deductive theory. These standards for research not only would devalue almost *all* processes of knowledge formation, but are cavalierly beside the point of the substantial differences between "action research" and "normal science."

This pall did not seem to afflict all equally. Many of the brothers and sisters with writer's itch had the affliction in serious degree. Even seasoned researchers, for example, were prone to see the "repudiation of all OD theory" in results that could be interpreted in many ways, most of which were more proximate and more reasonable alternatives than the cosmic conclusions that were so compelling to many. The day-to-day interveners seemed troubled by the temper of the times, but less affected. I recall one practitioner bursting out at a panel, intently focused on raising everyone's consciousness about how OD fell short of perfectibility: "Those guys are making all my constants into galloping variables."

The casual observer might easily have concluded that many contributors to the OD literature had a masochistic streak. Or perhaps they saw such a sorry record of success in OD interventions—their own records as well as of others, one must suppose—that the rush was on to point the accusing finger lest someone not in the lodge beat them to it. Or the more knowledgeable observer might have guessed that certain key studies were incautiously interpreted as establishing the general inappropriateness of OD technology,[1] or at least as indicating the sharp limits on the applicability of certain popular forms of that technology. Less charitable guesses also might be made, but to no useful end here.

However, dead certainty is appropriate on one point. That relates to the reaction of the doom-and-gloom crowd when a substantial set of studies became available about OD success rates.

A bit of stage-setting must precede attention to the ongoing reaction to new and contrary data. At least three major studies of success rates appeared in the interval 1979–82: Porras zeroed in on a large array of variables in a smallish population of studies deliberately chosen for the methodological rigor of their designs;[2] Golembiewski, Proehl, and Sink looked at 574 OD applications and estimated their impact on both "hard" and "soft" indicators;[3] and Nicholas focused solely on various "hard" indicators of performance in a small batch of studies with that crucial focus.[4]

The results? Approximations will have to do here but—since no close calls are required—the reliance on ballpark figures poses no major problems. The researchers use various criteria for "success," both global and specific, and one even required either statistically significant differences or improvements of at least 20 percent. The latter requirement staggers. What manager would not be overjoyed with a 20 percent improvement in any indicator? Or even 2 percent?

The reasons for setting high hurdles are plain enough, and although the "success ranges" varied somewhat, they did so in a very nice neighborhood. About 50 to 75 percent of all OD applications are rated as "successful" by the three separate studies, give or take a decimal here or there.

The reaction to these summary studies—or more precisely, the lack of a reaction to them—astounds. The handwringing has stopped, but there seems no clear replacement by the ex-handwringers for the pessimism that went unaffirmed. Silence is what there seems, mostly. No hurrahs for high success rates, and not even any critiques of scope and method of the assessment studies. Silence. Just silence. This improves on free-floating pessimism, but not much.

When data about success were in short supply, one can perhaps somewhat understand the pessimism in the literature and at professional meetings. I emphasize "perhaps somewhat understand." For even pre-1980, curiously, a batch of assessment studies had been available for years. Their success rates do not differ markedly from the three evaluative studies sketched above,[5] in addition, although the latter studies have several advantages over their predecessors. For whatever reasons, the earlier assessments did not much influence the worried tone of most of the OD literature.

The lack of affirmative response when the more recent batch of success rates became available is less easy to understand. Not only do those studies imply success rates with attractive orders of magnitude, but they have other advantages. Thus one focuses on a population of studies that is ten times larger than any other survey of applications. A second study focuses on only the most rigorous research designs which, one supposes, might well reduce the success rates observed, or at least increase one's confidence in any reported consequences of OD applications. And the third summary study deals only with "hard" outcomes, which have a special salience for both researchers and especially practitioners. In the bargain, this evaluative study sets very high standards for "success."

As I say, the lack of reaction to the evaluation literature always was curious. Its gets curiouser every day.

Why should those assessment studies, both early and more recent, have caused such a "plop"?

A flourish of trumpets would seem the more appropriate response, or at least a zinging critique.

Any ideas, anyone?

Notes

1. The Michigan ICL study no doubt had such a chilling effect, for example, although ways were found to reasonably limit early doomsday interpretations of the study's implications for OD technology. See David G. Bowers, "OD Techniques and Their Results in 23 Organizations," *Journal of Applied Behavioral Science* 9 (Jan. 1973): 21–43.

2. Jerry I. Porras, "The Comparative Impact of Different OD Techniques and Their Results in 23 Organizations," *Journal of Applied Behavioral Science* 15 (April 1979): 156–78.

3. Robert T. Golembiewski, Carl W. Proehl, and David Sink, "Estimating the Success of OD Applications," *Training and Development Journal* 72 (April 1982): 86–95. See also their "Success of OD Applications in the Public Sector," *Public Administration Review* 41 (Nov. 1981): 679–82.

4. John M. Nicholas, "The Comparative Impact of Organization Development Interventions on Hard Criteria Measures," *Academy of Management Review* 7 (Oct. 1982): 531–42.

5. For example, consult Newton Margulies, Penny L. Wright, and Richard W. Scholl, "Organization Development Techniques," *Group and Organization Studies* 2 (Dec. 1977): 428–48; Larry E. Pate, Warren R. Nielsen, and Paula C. Bacon, "Advances in Research on Organization Development," *Group and Organization Studies* 2 (Dec. 1977): 449–60; and Peggy Morrison, "Evaluation in OD," *Group and Organization Studies* 3 (March 1978): 42–70.

15

An Even Better-Kept Secret: Success Rates in Third-World Applications

Readers of the preceding thought pieces,[1] as well as of the literature on planned change,[2] will have a sense of my deep fascination with success rates. This interest relates not only to assessing the probability that intended consequences will follow from the application of specific OD techniques, as guided by OD values. Even more, I am intrigued by the all but universal lack of public reaction to the substantial (even formidable) success rates that have been reported.

What say these neglected assessments of OD applications? Criteria of "success" will vary, of course. But I know of no evaluative study that reports less than 50 percent "success," and the rate is typically in the 70 percent range.[3] In summary, the evaluation literature severely challenges the validity of three basic propositions in the common wisdom about OD, often espoused by ODers themselves:

- OD success rates in business organizations are nothing to write home about, although applications can be justified if the need is great and one is a high risk taker.
- OD success rates in government will be appreciably lower, if efforts there are not doomed to frustration.
- Indeed, so great are public-sector obstacles to OD said to be that few applications are even attempted in governmental settings.

The mounting evidence urged me on. What would the least-favorable conditions imply for OD efforts: impoverished countries, low-technology settings, and unsophisticated populations, for example?

The common wisdom provides a ready answer, only a few of whose major assumptions need to be outlined here. OD evolved in "developed" economies with quite specific features—high tech and high touch, to select convenient labels. OD activities can be costly and longer-range, in addition, and they might seem more applicable to "sophisticated" work forces. The reader can easily add length and breadth to this short list.

"Undeveloped" countries do not seem hospitable hosts for OD efforts, then. Their economies are low tech with unsophisticated work forces, and their commonly autocratic cultures suggest low (or distant) touch at work. We should expect few applications there, and those rarities should have low success rates.

This assumptive line seems quite reasonable, but it suffers from two liabilities. First, no one had sought to isolate a panel of such OD applications to test the assumptions. Second, when that effort was made recently, the results did not provide strong support for the common wisdom.

So let us back up a bit, providing context and detail for this search for OD applications in non-Western settings. Seven points outline the effort:[4]

1. The focus was on large political jurisdictions with 1980 GNP per capita below $5,000 U.S.

2. About sixty journals were searched, typically for a 30-year period; lists of dissertations and theses were examined; and about 100 ODers with Third-World connections were contacted for leads to published or unpublished applications.

3. How many OD efforts did this effort generate? Additions still trickle in, but the present panel contains eighty-two applications from thirty-six large political jurisdictions, very often countries or nations.

4. About two-thirds of the applications are from jurisdictions with per capita GNP 1980 of $1,500 U.S. or less.

5. The panel contains a broad range of application sites: large government projects, banks, small plants, newly literate and impoverished villagers, and so on.

6. There seem no appreciable differences in success rates between the several classes of sites.

7. The overall success rates are substantial, although lower than for a large panel of applications with a strong bias toward Western and developed settings. See Table 15.1.

Table 15.1

	82 Applications in Nonaffluent Settings	574 Applications in Western and Developed Settings
I Highly positive and intended effects	15%	40%
II Definite balance of positive and intended effects	55	47
III No appreciable effects	29	6
IV Negative effects	1	8

Say what about the common wisdom of the success rates in non-Western and Third-World settings.? Those rates seem an even better kept secret (or is it a surprise?) than the rates for more common settings.

Notes

1. "So, What About Success Rates?" *Organization Development Journal* 4 (Fall 1986): 5–6. See also "You Can't be a Beacon," I and II, in the two following numbers.
2. Robert T. Golembiewski, Carl W. Proehl, Jr., and David Sink, "Estimating the Success of OD Applications," *Training and Development Journal* 72 (April 1982): 86–95.
3. For reports of the lower range of success rates, see Jerry I. Porras, "The Comparative Impact of Different OD Techniques and Their Results . . . ," *Journal of Applied Behavioral Science* 15 (April 1979): 156–78; and John M. Nicholas, "The Comparative Impact of Organization Development Interventions on Hard Criteria Measures," *Academy of Management Review* 7 (Oct. 1982): 531–42.
4. Robert T. Golembiewski, "OD Applications in Non-Affluent Settings." Paper delivered at The International Conference on Organization Behavior and Development, Ahmedabad, India, December 29, 1986–January 3, 1987. This paper presents the data for seventy cases, which is here up-dated for eighty-two applications. The panel now has 100 applications, and no serious qualification of the discussion above is required. See Robert T. Golembiewski, "Is OD Narrowly Culture-Bound," *Organization Development Journal* 5 (Winter 1987): 20–29.

16

"We Are Not Here to Reinvent the Status Quo"

Every once in a while, all of us says something that sets the tone of an interchange, for good or ill. One of my favorites occurred at the very opening of what promised to be a tense meeting concerning the broad adoption of what had been a dramatically successful pilot study in R & D with a flexible work-hours intervention. The practical consequences were solidly positive;[1] and the theoretical follow-on work highlighted what seems a relevant issue in OD analysis and application.[2]

Despite the undoubted attractions, the diffusion of the flexible work-hours innovation was no slam dunk. This was one of the first large-scale U.S. applications, and the normal concerns about that year's management fad were much in the air. Also prominent was the injunction: Pilot studies often work, but large-scale applications are another matter entirely.

More to the point, I believe, organizational politics also loomed large. "We" were the OD guys and gals, armored not only with humanistic values but also in this case with solid data—gathered at several points in time, and even from a comparison group as well as the experimental unit. Those data indicated that flexible work hours were quite a good thing, for employees and management. "They" represented the more traditional HR functions, who were given to philosophical concerns about "giving away the store," as well as powerful cautions that "what worked in R & D won't necessarily work in marketing and manufacturing." Not publicly expressed, but always there, was a massive fact. "We" were spearheading an early Quality of Working Life (QWL) project, mandated by a CEO who deliberately bypassed almost all the other HR staff. The OD group—true to their espoused theory—struggled to get the CEO to change his mind on this crucial point, but without effect, and on two occasions came close to rejecting the CEO's mandate because of his exclusionary stance. "They" were informed about our efforts and preferences, but I'm certain "they" were generally unbelieving.

So the issues were clearly drawn, if politely. On the one hand stood the results of a pilot study that defied nit-picking, but nonetheless raised legitimate philosophical and practical issues about the kind of control for *this* organization at *that* specific time. On the other hand loomed the political interests. Most of HR had a reasonable concern about being bypassed in the QWL study; and the OD group was deliciously aware of the irony of beginning a collaborative program in a noncollaborative way, while also realizing that implementation of the QWL study would of necessity involve those very HR resources which the CEO mandated out of the planning, research, and recommendation phases. While vigorously warning the CEO, and even almost deciding to refuse the CEO's mandate, the OD group decided to move on— albeit by a split decision, and while informing other HR folks of the double bind, of the OD counter preferences, and of action steps the QWL team contemplated. "Well, what would you do in our place?" summarized the OD view presented to others in HR.

Hence the importance of that particular meeting between HR managers and the OD group. Results of the QWL pilot study with a flexible work-hours program would be reviewed in detail, and two goals would dominate. First, discussion would center around whether HR would join in spirit in the favorable recommendation by the QWL team to extend flexible work hours. Second, discussion would explore the related issue of HR's views concerning implementation—willingness to help, appropriate strategies, possible problems, and so on.

The premeeting talk bustled with the electricity of opposed interests-in-the-air. But some opening remarks had a galvanizing effect: "Gentlemen, we are not here to reinvent the status quo." That put our agendas and our focus in a usefully different perspective. We all tried to rise to *the* situation and to the *common* challenge.

Why retell that story? Now is a very good time to use that line again: ". . . we are not here to reinvent the status quo."

There is *no best place* to use that line. But there seems *a very good place* to do so nowadays.

Specifically, I have reference to the poor, economically disadvantaged, and culturally deprived, as well as to OD's record in dealing directly with them. In sum, that record is not only sorry, *but it is also getting worse*. After a brief flurry of activity in the mid-1960s and early 1970s, visible signs of such interventions have all but disappeared.

Let me rely on the best evidence of which I know, which has its weaknesses but supports the present point with plenty to spare. The focus was restricted to "developed countries"—specifically those with 1980 per capita GNPs of $5,000 U.S. or more. There are thirty-eight such countries.[3]

For those thirty-eight countries, two selective criteria were applied in seeking OD applications dealing directly with the disadvantaged. What defines our target? An OD application to the managerial staff of a people-helping agency *does not* count. An OD application to the migrant workers in a fruit-picking operation *does* qualify, even though those workers are employed by an agribusiness that is funding the effort. Over thirty journals were searched for twenty-five years, and approximately 100 experienced intervenors were contacted concerning leads to cases that have been committed to writing.

What do we learn from that population of OD cases? Three points must suffice for present purposes.

- First, pitifully few cases exist. Concerted efforts were made to find cases, but with little effect. Published and unpublished sources were solicited. The number found in this search: thirty-seven cases, in all!
- Second, *almost all* of the OD applications occurred during the years of urban turmoil following the deaths of Dr. King and President Kennedy. Put another way, a paltry 5 percent of the total number of OD applications involving the disadvantaged occurred in the last eight years.
- Third, low success rates *do not* explain the almost total recent neglect. In fact, the success rates are tolerable, compared to a population of 574 OD applications that mostly deal with elites in public and business organizations. See Table 16.1.

Table 16.1

	Success-Rate Estimates, in %	
	37 Cases with Economically Disadvantaged Populations	574 OD Applications
I Definite balance of intended effects	8%	41%
II Balance of intended effects	68	46
III No effects	16	6
IV Negative unintended effects	8	7

There is nothing morally superior about intervening for either the powerless or the powerful. Thus the careless or ethically unconscious ODer can labor only to cool out those low in economic power. Or such and ODer can sell out to the economically powerful, consciously or just conveniently.

But it appears to me that a greater balance has something to recommend it, in the abstract. Working with the economically powerless is a good place to raise that reorienting clarion call: ". . . we are not here to reinvent the status quo." Indeed, it may be substantially the case that such a call cannot be raised anywhere very effectively until it guides a substantial number of applications in deprived settings.

Notes

1. Robert T. Golembiewski, Richard Hilles, and Munro Kagno, "A Longitudinal Study of Flexi-Time Effects," *Journal of Applied Behavioral Science* 10 (Sept. 1974): 405–17.
2. Robert T. Golembiewski, Keith Billingsley, and Samuel Yeager, "Measuring Change and Persistence in Human Affairs," *Journal of Applied Behavioral Science* 12 (June 1976): 133–57.
3. Robert T. Golembiewski, "OD Applications in Economically-Deprived Settings," *Public Administration Quarterly* (in press).

17

"You Can't Be a Beacon . . . ," I

Truth is where you find it, of course. And it is in that context that my attention was attracted to a recent emphasis on the religious shows that are strung all along the radio dials in the southeastern states, and no doubt elsewhere as well. A spritely song encourages evangelizing and proselytizing for Christ, joyfully, and proposes as its punch line that:

> You can't be a beacon
> if your light don't shine!

The sentiment is not new, to be sure. A classical colleague reminds me that Plato said much the same thing in his advice about how to live the only life worth living—that of thoughtful and enlightened activism. Don't hide your lantern under a basket, Plato advised those intent on living the just life and leading others to do the same.

Plato and the radio evangelizers notwithstanding, the preceding selections—"So, What About Success Rates?" and "An Event Better Kept Secret," and "We Are Not Here to Reinvent the Status Quo . . ."—focus on the curious behavior of Organization Development specialists. These women and men are devotees of what should be a thoughtful and enlightened activism in connection with cooperative effort, but they have been moot concerning accumulating evidence that success rates in OD are not at all bad—indeed, viewed in different ways by a range of observers, these success rates range from good to excellent.[1] Even the relatively negative reviews are substantially positive, with the lowest success rates approximating 50 percent.

We still lack critical fine tuning, to be sure. For example, we do not have evidence about the proportion of "natural improvements," of spontaneous healings, if you will. But that implies no need to cry hunger with a loaf of bread under your arm. Even 50 percent ain't bad, lacunae and all.

Circumstances make the silence even more of a curiosity. Numerous observers had over the years called for just such summary evaluations, for one thing, all the better to separate the wheat from the chaff so as to enhance the aptness and impact of OD designs and programs of change. Now the evidence is becoming increasingly available, and not only does it seem to be favorable evidence—on definite balance—but it has come at a time when some influential voices are concerned that OD is a "maturing market" and hence is in danger of falling into the shoddy practices common when the supply of resources outstrips the demand for them. Native cunning urges taking advantage of the news about success rates, in short, all the better to stimulate demand and hence to help avoid the grim dynamics of "maturing markets."

And yet the silence about success rates persists. ODers clearly are not letting their faces light up as they refer to substantial success rates, and hence OD is less likely to be a beacon for those in collective distress.

An earlier editorial asked help of the readers. Did they have any ideas that might help explain what seems on the face of it a strange and even paradoxical state of affairs? This editorial and a following one distill some of the main themes of reader responses, as well as some second or third thoughts of my own. Hence there will be two editorials on why ODers have not been a beacon for their specialty because their faces do not shine with confidence about favorable success rates. This editorial is "You Can't Be a Beacon . . . ," I, and it will be complemented and reinforced by—of course—II.

Before we start, let us admit one possibility. High success rates have a forbidding character—a thorn among the roses, as it were. Such rates heighten expectations, and hence imply greater psychological loss when failure occurs. If that is our problem, well, we will just have to learn how to live with raising the ante. Beyond this possibility, Beacon I focuses on a single if involved point: why both OD "optimists" and "pessimists" might have given the silent treatment to the success-rate literature. Beacon II adds four additional speculative reasons, which are more direct that Beacon I's contribution.

Obviously, the silence might well derive from a reasonable caution that the results are spurious or somehow artifactual. Observers can come to this conclusion in two different ways, however. Let us distinguish two classes of ODers responding to the growing literature on success rates—those who had an interest in the matter but whose minds were still open as to the results of aggregate analysis of successes/failures in individual studies; and those who had already made up their minds on the matter, and who reflected a public pessimism about success rates. This latter camp all but dominated the literature and conferences, taking two strong (if curious for ODers) positions that organizational success rates are modest, and particularly in the public service.

Parenthetically, one wonders why the pessimists kept doing what they did—that is, OD. Given really low success rates, the obvious needs doing: Back to the drawing board!

But I digress.

Now, how might silence be the reaction of these two classes of ODers? No one can say for sure, of course, but speculation is encouraged by the silence, even required by it.

Well, for openers, the open-minded ODers might be responding with conservative caution, perhaps born of unhappy experiences with too little restrained exuberances of the past. Sure enough, there have been "major findings" that were soon enough variously deflated, if not punctured beyond all hope of repair.

This view about open-minded ODers encourages two reactions, primarily. Thus it may be edifying to contemplate such a collection of sedulous waiters on the future, relying on the processes of analysis and critique to generate some substantially correct approximation of a working truth, while the world continues to turn. It may be edifying, as I noted, but this view makes too much of a good thing—that is, patience while truth-values get tested, and hence variously qualified or even rejected. It has been *a long time* since a second freshet of evaluation studies began appearing in late 1981 and then in greater numbers in 1982 and 1983. And it has been longer still since an earlier batch of evaluation studies appeared in the mid to late 1970s.

The ODers who had come to pessimistic (and public) conclusions about low success rates, and especially in the public sector, seem to constitute an easier case in some senses. But that case nevertheless poses some subtle issues.

First crack out of the box, how would you behave if you had taken a position—often and rock-solid—that seemed to be substantially off-base, to judge from several evaluative studies? Silence is a reasonable enough reaction, and for several possible motives that might be working alone or in various combinations. Hence silence might be motivated by watchful waiting for contradictory evidence that others might supply. Or silence might simply be the outward sign of an industriousness devoted to developing a careful critique of the evaluation studies, or even to generate data supporting the contrary point. Or silence for the public pessimists might simply reflect a reasonable hunkering down—a kind of CYA by looking elsewhere, hard. During this period of active neglect, the mass of ODers at least would be less likely to have the evaluative literature impressed on their minds by vigorous debate. Alternatively or complementarily, the watchful OD public might come to forget who had made which pessimistic assessments about success rates, in the absence of an enthusiasm about success-rate findings from past pessimists or, indeed, in the absence of any mention at all.

All well and good for purposes of stimulating thought, perhaps, but the pessimistic camp also encourages subtler analysis. Consider here only the issue that nobody likes to have their baby called ugly, and any concerted attention to the emerging success-rates literature would perforce call attention to the uncomeliness *of someone's baby*.

Some details are useful. Without naming names, the success-rate literature nonetheless raised direct questions about the conclusions of the public pessimists that OD success rates were quite low, and especially in the public sector. But that challenge was implicit rather than direct, and the pessimists might have decided against drawing attention to the challenge, even if they considered it poorly founded. Of course, direct and telling criticism of the evaluative literature also could blunt the implied but direct criticism, and perhaps destroy it.

These possibilities encompass a subtle wrinkle. In one case, a well-known ODer was developing the point that the record of change in large bureaucracies seemed a sorry one, with the exception of several of my publications. Burke notes:[2] "Robert Golembiewski is one of the more experienced consultants in the field of OD with bureaucracies, especially in the public sector. He tends to be optimistic about such consultation. . . . To the extent that he is successful as a consultant, he may be an exception to my remarks about . . . OD in the public sector. Most OD consultants find working with bureaucracies, especially public ones, to be difficult at best. . . ."

The common extension of this position to all OD created a kind of cul-de-sac for OD pessimists in relation to the emerging success-rate literature. To put the implied point in its boldest terms, the substantial success rates left only uncomfortable conceptual territory for the pessimists. Their once-dominant view could now be cast as an exception to general practice, an exception which could have roots—to cite the major but not exclusive possibilities—either in the somehow peculiarly difficult situations that pessimists encountered or in the character and quality of their OD consultation.

Such a conceptual tight fit might well encourage silence. For it would be difficult to establish that the pessimists had somehow selected the noneasy pieces for intervening, in general. Moreover, precious little motivation would exist among pessimists to embrace the second possibility.

Notes

1. The success-rate literature came in two general waves. The earlier evaluations of batches of OD applications include: Newton Margulies, Penny L. Wright, and Richard W. Scholl, "Organizational Development Techniques," *Group and Organization Studies* 2 (Dec. 1977): 428; and Larry E. Pate, Warren R. Nielsen, and Paul C. Bacon, "Advances in Research on Organization Development," *Group and Organization Studies* 2 (Dec. 1977): 449–60. The more recent wave includes larger batches of applications and/or more strict criteria of success. These studies include: Robert T. Golembiewski, Carl W. Proehl, Jr., and David Sink, "Estimating the Success of OD Applications," *Training and Development Journal* 72 (April 1982): 86–95; John M. Nicholas, "The Comparative Impact of Organization Development Interventions on Hard Criteria Measures," *Academy of Management Review* 7 (Oct. 1982): 531–42; and D. E. Terpstra, "Evaluating Selected Organization Development Interventions," *Journal of Applied Psychology* 66 (1981): 541–43.
2. W. Warner Burke, "Organization Development and Bureaucracy in the 1980s," *Journal of Applied Behavioral Science* 16 (Sept. 1980): 428–29.

18

"You Can't Be a Beacon . . . ," II

"You Can't Be a Beacon . . . , I," dwelt on a single if involved speculation about why the emerging success-rate literature has inspired so little contention or even apparent interest. That selection elaborates on the elemental
notion that "You can't be a beacon if your light don't shine." Why ODers did
not seize on the success literature—to have their faces shine about favorable
success rates so as to be a beacon directing users to OD—constitutes the heart
of the speculative demonstration that the earlier editorial initiates, and this
editorial concludes.

Basically, "Beacon I" distinguishes two clusters of ODers prominent in
published materials and in professional conferences. A small cohort reflected
an optimism about success rates for OD applications, and especially in the
public sector; and the larger and dominant chorus of pessimists took the contrary position. The first editorial suggests why both optimists and pessimists
may have given an underwhelming response to the emerging success-rate literature.

"Beacon II" adds four points to the beginning made in "Beacon I" of a
possible explanation of the curious silence.

First, and perhaps an issue that might have been better disposed of in Beacon I, the success rate literature may be perceived as shoddy and
unconvincing, more or less by all. And that could have inspired silence, obviously. Thus optimists would not attack that literature because they believed in
its basic premise, but they could not bring themselves to support the literature
because it was so halt and lame. And pessimists might have inwardly reveled
in the literature's multiple inelegancies, because they did not accept its basic
premise. The pessimists might have opted to let that literature simply "twist
slowly in the wind," hanging as a gaunt reminder that its component studies
and their inept research designs were their own worst enemy.

This is possible, of course, but not credible. White House staffers might
generate such restraint, but such behavior in ODers is simply not believable.
After all, ODers are specialists in openness and confrontation. Reticence
might affect individuals among them, of course; and loyalties and friendships
might mask some reactions, as happens at least occasionally with Everyman.
However, I simply cannot visualize silence, had even a determined few

concluded—be they previous pessimists or optimists—that the success-rate literature is defective or dumb in design or details.

Of course, I have a vested interest here. As a contributor to the success-rate literature, this is a reasonable position for me to take. Hence I emphasize the possibility that my position is reasonably mistaken, with judgement being dulled by too many hours assembling, with others, 574 applications so as to see what they had to say about success rates.

Second, success rates may be widely seen by ODers as largely beside the point, if not an absolute drag. Hence silence merely gives that literature what it so fully deserves, from this perspective.

Now, what can this second point mean, beyond a veiled reference to the sometimes monumental counterdependence of some ODers? Let us see.

This second position can claim some support, in fact, given a bit of analytic license. Thus OD often puts a premium on spontaneity and involvement. Some even have proposed that there is no such thing as an ineffective learning design: there are only designs that people accept or identify with more or less strongly. For such a belief, evaluation is worse than beside the point, because the success-rate literature tends to focus on the relative potency of classes of designs. As such, the success-rate literature may draw attention away from the critical processes, perhaps even perverting them in a naive search for certainty about specific designs when only (or mostly) the basic processes are relevant—participation and involvement. Rather than assessing the relative success rates of classes of designs, that is, the focus should be unrelievedly on how to do well in inducing participation and involvement. That induction being accomplished, success rates will take care of themselves.

Bluntly put, from this view a "failure" is an insufficient engagement of participation and involvement, which generate inadequate owning. And this "failure" is likely to reflect on individual intervenors, awkward situational features, in specific cases, or just plain bad luck. Moreover, the specific learning designs do not much effect what happens, in this view; or alternatively, the designs and their associated dynamics are so diverse and unique as to defy classification. Hence the success-rate approach diverts attention rather than helps.

A polar-opposite view also can be nestled quite comfortably in this second point, which devalues the activity of evaluating success rates. Specifically, some ODers may be convinced that the present phase of their area's development should emphasize the assemblage of a "critical mass" of adherents sufficient to do useful things near and dear to their hearts—to help create an escape velocity sufficient for the development of a full-blown profession, to help build demand for OD services, or whatever.

For people with such a view of immediate developmental priorities, even talk about success rates could be counterproductive. For each design or approach that "works," in short, there may be designs/approaches that do not work. So success rates have exclusionary as well as inclusionary effects, and this duality poorly serves the interest of those intent largely on achieving some critical mass for OD. This tension—as it were, between getting as many people as possible under the tent, as opposed to checking tickets closely—has appeared in various forms in OD, particularly in the issue of professional certification. Generally, so far, the ticket checkers have not prevailed.

We need not look hard for major examples of this disinclination to rain on any part of a growing OD parade, I believe. This conclusion may be a strictly personal one, but it seems to me that a kind of cottage industry has developed to facilitate the expansion of "OD" to comfortably include broad ranges of folk and ideas. The Organization Development Network has played a major role of this kind, for example, and I reckon the consequences as generally positive.

At times, however, cross-purposes meet themselves coming around the same corner. To illustrate, part of the pessimism about OD derives from popularizations and metaphors that poke fun at OD institutions and processes. The ready audience for such materials, I assume, comes in part from the healthy tendency to look at one's self and work whimsically and iconoclastically. The appetite for such business is so persisting and so great, however, that I assume a substantial part of motivation for it must come from the large proportion of new hands in OD, a characteristic not only of early stages of growth of OD but also of the short tours of duty "in OD" in many organizations. These large proportions of short-timers not only need to be made aware of progress and especially pitfalls, but particularly in nonthreatening ways. There are no better forms for such learning than the artful play on words that engages more than it illuminates as it teases and tests, or the humorous metaphor whose lack of discrimination can be pardoned because its apparent spirit is playful and unserious, even hilarious. I have in mind here efforts that relate to "Phrog Pharms" with its not so subtle digs at earned and learned degrees, "Wizards of OD," and the like.

Without being an old grouch, and without seeking to rain on anyone's parade or charade, the effects of such efforts have to be reckoned in terms of both pluses and minuses. They are good for a laugh. But such metaphors or plays on words are difficult to tether, especially for the partially aware.

Third, the literature on success rates may simply have come at an awkward time—if for different reasons for two relatively distinct clusters of ODers. Consider those interested in greater quality control over what OD is and who does it; and consider also those interested in expanding the demand for OD services. Of course, sometimes the same person will be counted in both clusters, at least on some issues. But typically a choice has to be made, for the two priorities often are at odds. In effect, OD has its more or less permanent supply-siders as well as its demand-siders.

For those intent on greater quality control—the supply-siders—now is an awkward time for trumpheting the good news about substantial success rates. And hence, perhaps their silence. Specifically, QC advocates have weathered the first major expansion and then contraction of the OD market, which cycle has only just been completed. The contracting demand no doubt forced out some marginal performers, or at least the less committed. Moreover, substantial progress has been made recently on raising the standards for OD performers, and especially by the recent announcement and broad discussion of a code of ethics, in which the Organization Development Institute played such an important motivating and nurturing role. Much remains to be done, however. For example, the code will at first be voluntary or advisory, and only later will it become part of a conscious professional filtering process for those in/out of OD. See also selection 26, Part III.

From the supply-side perspective, then, this is the wrong time to encourage a rush of new would-be ODers into the fold. Times for that will be more propitious when the standards in the code of ethics have become more understood and accepted. In fact, a sudden influx of OD recruits might even jeopardize the very recent progress made toward a code of ethics. This implies risks for the greater downstream QC that the code is intended to facilitate.

But what of the silence of those whose definite priority goes to enlarging demand—the demand-siders? One would think they, if anybody, would be intent on spreading the gospel of favorable success rates, which should motivate greater reliance on OD resources.

Let's try to outline a rationale for the more curious demand-side silence. The success-rate literature has a dual potential for demand-siders, for reasons already sketched, and hence that literature might be approached with care rather than embraced by those who focus on the demand side of OD. That is, any evaluative literature has implications for designs of choice or contraindicated designs. One cannot accept the market-enhancing possibilities of substantial success rates, in short, without buying into their real potential for goring one's favored ox.

Such effects are not merely possible. An early evaluative effort had precisely such a double-edged effect, in fact. Successful OD efforts in large organizations are possible, that research seemed to say, but not with the design that most ODers favored. Here the term "favored" refers not only to personal preferences, but also to an acceptance rooted in experience with appropriate skills and attitudes.[1] Similarly, I have observed an underwhelming interest among ODers about our ongoing work with burnout,[2] in part (at least) because it has a kind of triple whammy going against it, as most ODers see the world. Thus the research implies that advanced phases of burnout might not be remedial via the interaction designs favored by many ODers. Moreover, the choice between standard designs—on the face of existing research—might well require prior knowledge of degrees of burnout in host populations,[3] and such prework is not common. Finally, the phase approach to burnout raises serious concerns about reliance on "stress-management workshops"—which is perhaps *the* intervention of choice for stress or burnout.

Hence demand-siders also might be encouraged to silence about the success-rate literature. And this despite the danger that lack of criticism might imply agreement.

Fourth, a final possibility needs acknowledging for present purposes. The silence re success rates may in some measure derive from the learning style dominant among ODers. That is, they may dominantly be "oral and aural learners," for whom "the literature" has neither high nor credible status. Learning directly from experience—both immediate but also long-run—is no doubt a major contributor to an ODers' success. It may be just that—in the matter of the success-rate literature—this learned capacity works itself out as a delay in what might be called "learning by reading."

This fourth possibility includes some wicked features, for "direct learning" about success rates is limited by two factors. Thus all of us have limited experiences, no matter how active we are. More troublesome, "failure" may be tough to recognize, especially when long-run effects are involved. Moreover, our direct experience of failure is a composite of our own performance and of the designs we utilize. Hence personal judgment about success rates often will be contaminated by any tendency to see problems in the design when they were in some part problems in our own performance.

Notes

1. See David G. Bowers, "OD Techniques and their Results in 23 Organizations: The Michigan ICL Study," *Journal of Applied Behavioral Science* 9 (Sept. 1973): 21–43. For critiques of the reach-and-grasp of Bowers' work, see: William R. Torbert, "Some Questions on Bowers' Study of Different OD Techniques," *Journal of Applied Behavioral Science* 9 (Sept. 1973): 668–71; and William A. Pasmore, "The Michigan ICL Study Revisited: An Alternative Explanation of Results," *Journal of Applied Behavioral Science* 12 (June 1976): 245–51.
2. Robert T. Golembiewski, Robert F. Munzenrider, and Jerry Stevenson, *Stress in Organizations* (New York: Praeger, 1985).
3. Robert T. Golembiewski, "Enriching the Theory and Practice of Team-Building: Instrumentation for Diagnosis and Alternative for Design," 98–113, in D. D. Warrick, ed., *Contemporary Organization Development* (Glenview, Ill.: Scott, Foresman, 1985).

19

Is QWL OD's Charge? Or Vice Versa? Why It Matters Who Gets Custody

Custody disputes in natural families can be sad, even tragic; but the "custody" of disciplines or areas of work can be even more perplexing. In the former case, the key question is: which parent gets custody, and what are the visiting rights? For disciplines, added complexity typically must be dealt with. There, the issues typically involve judgments about which is parent, and which the child.

So it is with OD and QWL, or Quality of Working Life. This piece reviews some of the factors that led each to go its own ways, in critical regards, even as common pathways also were trod. Moreover, this piece offers an opinion about why it matters which is seen as parent and which as child. Or if that metaphor displeases, the point can be framed as well in terms of leading or following roles. Finally, this opinional essay also sketches reasons why QWL becoming OD's charge presents no great conceptual difficulties, practical problems aside for the moment. The reverse situation presents substantial difficulties, both to me and (I believe) in basic concept.

Let us begin with two thumbnail comparative histories.

For a variety of reasons, OD was begotten with a dominant emphasis on interaction, but with a substantial minority proposing that structures and policies/procedures also had to be taken into early (even primary) account in any comprehensive effort to act on OD values. (See also the earlier essay "OD As Stool: Ruminations About a Metaphor.")

The experiences of many early OD intervenors were rooted in process analysis and more specifically in T-Groups, which goes a long way toward explaining their dominant emphasis on interaction and human relationships. In most OD formulations, then, the front-load proposes that appropriate cultures need to be induced at work. Derivatively, these typical formulations note that suitable structures and sets of policies/procedures then will be generated by the general normative agreement as well as by the particular character of the cultures in specific organizations. For various historic reasons that aid and abet this emphasis on face-to-face interaction, OD also typically focused on executive or managerial levels, rather than on the workaday world. As one consequence, the OD literature not only contains little about operating levels, but it deals even less with unions or organized employees.

This top-down bias of OD contrasts sharply with the bottom-up developmental pattern of QWL. For diverse reasons, QWL has focused on operating levels in industrial or manufacturing settings, and thus has often dealt with unionized contexts. In substantial part, this is due to the importance of European settings in the development of QWL. We illustrate with a few aspects of this "European connection." "Sociotechnical" approaches got early attention in Europe, and such approaches are central in QWL. Moreover, "industrial democracy" got its earliest forceful expression in Europe, and especially in the Scandinavian countries, where ties with the trade-union movement are strong and where sociotechnical approaches often provide the model for attempted linkages between work and political philosophy.

These QWL similarities are significant, but QWL efforts are not peas in a pod. While both American and European QWL often focused on forms of job enrichment, European experience often sought extensions beyond the workplace, as in participation in policy making. Generally, also, job enrichment in the U.S. got its early major impetus from management, while its unions focused on wage and fringes rather than on the character of work.

Despite some basic differences in orientation, OD and QWL are not entirely ships on separate seas. Thus one of the earliest and most comprehensive OD ventures paid substantial attention to the design of work at the operating level,[1] but this was one of a few exceptions to the general rule. Later OD practice seems somewhat broader, however.[2] Relatedly, some QWL efforts were conducted in union-free settings and extended to all levels of a substantial corporation.[3] Moreover, OD figures were among the early proponents of job enrichment strategies, autonomous groups, and other QWL prominences.[4]

Essentially, nonetheless, the twain meet too seldom. This implies losses for both camps, unfortunately. Thus the rolls of ODers are full of individuals with interaction-centered interests and skills; while QWLers number among their members a large majority with job design and system-analytic skills. This recreates in another guise the prototypical separation of those concerned about people from those busy with designing jobs and structuring them in networks of authority and responsibility. This version of the human/technical dichotomy is no more satisfactory than other similar separations—between personnel departments and industrial engineering, and so on. Just as there is plenty of evidence that interaction-centered efforts have foundered because of the failure to reinforce strong employee preferences with suitable structures and policies/procedures, so also does evidence establish that even high levels of job design skills can lead to awkward consequences in the absence of appropriate behavior/attitudes and a supporting culture.[5]

So QWL and OD cannot be suffered to live apart, forever. Each has too much to offer the other; and each orientation is insufficient in itself. And this inevitably raises *the* issue—which approach is engine and which is caboose?

For this one person, and especially given American practice, there is no doubt about this issue. Basically, QWL in American tends not be disciplined by a consistent set of values. So QWL applications can cover a very broad range, but with a definite tendency to emphasize narrow efficiency.

This position requires some detailing. QWL has its normative philosophers and theoreticians,[6] to be sure, but for various reasons the QWL movement has neither a distinctive nor generally accepted basis in values. For one thing, QWL's normative predispositions—when they are expressed—are quite similar to those current in OD. Indeed, they are in general indistinguishable from them.[7] Moreover, numerous QWL efforts were (and are) OD efforts in all but superficial terminology, and overtly rely on much work clearly labeled as OD.[8] In addition, for the run-of-the-mill application, QWL reflects a less adequate linkage between preaching and practice than does OD. In part, this is due to the fact that by and large the QWL ideologists are often not intervenors but researchers or commentators. This contrasts sharply with OD, where far less role specialization exists along the practice/prescription interface. Relatedly, many QWL practitioners come from traditions—classical industrial consultation, industrial engineering, and so on—in which normative issues get little explicit attention, if they are not neglected or deliberately avoided.[9]

More generally, QWL ideology seems to have less direct influence on its practice than is the case in OD. Anyone who has doubts on this point should (for example) attend and compare an Organization Development Network meeting with the several public QWL forums. The contrasts will be less marked, for obvious reasons, for those few QWL ventures supported by NTL, the OD Network, or University Associates. For the bulk of QWL ventures, however, the contrasts with OD will be sharp and revealing on the issue of the degree of explicit normative tethering. For example, this is the case with the practitioner-dominated American Productivity Managers' Association, whose emphasis is on narrow efficiency.

In sum, a strong tendency exists for QWL applications to be either indistinguishable from OD efforts or to be unguided missiles, from a normative point of view. A vignette illustrates the latter tendency. Evaluation studies have found it necessary to distinguish QWL job enrichment efforts in two classes—as those with employee and supervisory participation, and those without it. In effect, "without" applications represent an autocratic imposition of a design for enlarging employee freedom and responsibility! Curiously, the need to make that distinction *is apparently considered unremarkable*, as is the fact that the "with" and "without" applications are approximately equal in number. That these studies show major differences favoring the "with participation" variety does not surprise. Value-sensitive applications of job enrichment would have raised the odds of success, but QWL ideologies—despite their attention to normative issues—provide insufficient tethering for practitioners. Here the normative mornings of OD can be of critical help.

This linkage of QWL to OD is conceptually an easy one, in fact, for at least two basic reasons. First, substantial correspondences exist between the *espoused values* of OD and QWL, to use Argyris' distinction. A leading role for OD is justified by its greater emphasis on those values, and by its firmer linkage of espousal to practice.

Second, quite a number of practitioners already work both sides of the OD/QWL street, in effect seeing only a pair of major differences between the two approaches—in their usual level of application, and in the leading mode of intervention. Moreover, these differences complement one another, and each implies the usefulness of linking with the other. Consider two points:

- OD often begins at or near the top of an organization and typically leads off with interaction-centered designs; but comprehensive OD applications not only need to be extended throughout an organization, but with ample reliance on interventions that focus on structures and policies/procedures.
- QWL often begins with the operational levels of an organization, and the initial emphasis is on the design of jobs, and also on the specification of structural arrangements as well as on suitable policies and procedures. However, QWL applications with more than episodic ambitions must begin to deal with patterns of human relationships and appropriate cultures at work. Witness the work under the QWL banner that designs high-involvement plants,[10] in which the character of personal relationships and the work culture have very prominent places.

So the OD-QWL linkage should not prove a wrenching experience for proponents of either historic approach, at least conceptually. Some ODers and QWLers, in fact, have made the linkage all along. Moreover, the view of OD sketched in an earlier section—"OD As Stool: Ruminations on a Metaphor"—provides a congenial vehicle for this linkage. Here, QWL activities as usually practiced would be especially represented in two of the three legs of the OD stool—structures and policies/procedures.

Notes

1. Alfred J. Marrow, David G. Bowers, and Stanley E. Seashore, *Management by Participation* (New York: Harper & Row, 1967).
2. Consult John Nicholas, "The Comparative Impact of Organization Development Interventions on Hard Criteria Measures," *Academy of Management Review* 7 (Oct. 1982): 531–42.

3. Eg. Stokes B. Carrigan, "OD in Pharmaceutical Industry," 48–68, in H. Jennings Partain, ed. *Current Perspectives in Organization Development* (Reading, Mass.: Addison–Wesley, 1973).

4. E.g., Chris Argyris, *Behavior and Organization* (New York: Harper, 1957); and Robert T. Golembiewski, *Men, Management and Morality* (New York: McGraw-Hill, 1965).

5. See Paul H. Mirvis and D. N. Berg, *Failures in Organization Development and Change* (New York: Wiley, 1977).

6. Consult J. R. Hackman and V. C. Suttle, editors, *Improving Life at Work* (Santa Monica, Cal.: Goodyear Publishing, 1977), 1–25.

7. Ben-chu Sun, *The Impact of QWL Programs*. Unpublished doctoral dissertation, University of Georgia, 1988, Chaps I and II.

8. See, for example, Peter F. Sorenson, Jr., Thomas C. Head, and Dick Stotz, "Quality of Work Life in the Small Organization," *Group and Organization Change* 10 (Sept. 1985): 320–39.

9. The point holds especially for those associated with "scientific management." See Robert T. Golembiewski, *Behavior and Organization* (Chicago: Rand McNally, 1962), esp. Chaps 1 and 2.

10. Dennis N. T. Perkins, Veronica F. Nieva, and Edward E. Lawler, III, *Managing Creation* (New York: Wiley, 1983).

20

Judas Goats and Providing or Withholding Consultation

This piece emphasizes an old chestnut—when to provide OD consultation, and when to withhold it from a client—whose discussion is good for sharpening distinctions as well as for providing advance warnings about personal and professional dilemmas. Just how old is this particular chestnut? I recall that in the late 1960s convention-goers debated whether an OD consultant should provide services to organized crime, if approached. And I read in the Bible that Jethro also had concerns about consulting with Moses, who was having troubles with desert treks and associated logistics.

The issues are much the same whether the consultee is organized crime, the Ku Klux Klan, a firm manufacturing napalm during the Vietnam war, the Nazis during World War II, or some other client whose motives and especially behavior are substantially suspect. Two extreme models anchor the range for debate and choice. At one extreme, the OD intervenor is encouraged to be very vigilant in assessing the behaviors and motives of potential clients, judging some as worthy and rejecting others as somehow deficient. The opposed model emphasizes being of service, in both negative and positive senses. Negatively, this view proposes that the OD intervenor should get on with doing what is required, when asked or perhaps even when the client cannot really ask. Motives and behavior are for someone else to judge, in this view, on the general order of a medical doctor suddenly confronted with an accident victim. Positively, this view also suggests that OD services are socially valuable and intervenors therefore should make them available, more or less regardless. An exemplar of this perspective is the lawyer serving a person indicted for a crime. The lawyer's focus is not on innocence or guilt, but on the broader purpose of contributing to everyone else's freedom by making it as difficult as possible for legal authorities to convict the indictee.

In my own thinking about this torturous and crucial subject, I find it convenient to think of ''Judas goats'' and ''value complementarity.'' Briefly, paying attention to the latter can help the OD consultant from being one of the former.

This and the following bit of opinion will consider each of those aids to thinking and deciding about when to proffer and when to withhold OD services. "Judas goats" and "value complementarity" do not settle the vexing issues of providing/withholding services, but they do constitute aids for thought and action.

What does it mean to be a Judas goat? Abattoirs at one time used Judas goats, and perhaps still do. These animal stooges of slaughterhouse officialdom would serve to calm the other animals being led to their final fate, leading them to the electric shocks of insensibility and to the knife that severs jugulars. For their service, Judas goats were spared these final ministrations, for the time being.

It is not flattering or even pleasant to think of Judas goats in connection with OD interventions, of course, but that is precisely my reason for proposing the metaphor. The goal is to inhibit Judas goatship, as it were. Consequently, the less attractive the metaphor, the more aversion may be encouraged. Or that is the present hope, at least.

There are two basic defenses available to ODers against Judas goatship. The first is a diligent attention to the maxim that OD intervenors should emphasize creating choices and an awareness of them, as opposed to triggering or forcing change. Beyond that, consultant is well advised to mobilize an energetic inquisitiveness and even wonder about what clients seem to want, and why. This orientation often gets expressed in what I can only call "native cunning," a kind of street smarts applicable to organizational life. You get those messages in your consultant's antennae, and the processes provide support for the view that the consultant's most powerful tool is her or his "warm body."

In some cases, this concern about client's intent can be expressed quite directly, as in my common query when I am asked to do some team building. "Are there any walking wounded among the participants?" I am programmed to ask, by which I mean persons "on warning" or otherwise in jeopardy. If there are, I get very inquisitive about why action has not been taken, if the adverse case seems sufficient. And I typically recommend that negative personnel actions be taken prior to the team building. My intent is transparent. Such walking wounded often are a trial for everyone, themselves included, and their common nonperson status merely obscures and confuses. So part of my intent is to seek to increase the probability of success, as well as to avoid such awkward outcomes as the possible hostility or misplaced sympathy that other participants might develop for the vulnerable member during a team-building experience. Moreover, more than one "team-building session" has been the brainchild of managers without the moxie to do what they have long concluded needs doing. They hope "the team" will serve as a kind of "hit squad" or consortium of organizational executioners to do the deed, or to encourage it mightily. My intent is to avoid supporting, let alone participating in, such a cruel charade and shirking of managerial responsibility.

Now, to make the record perfectly plain, I do *not* believe that many (or even any) OD intervenors would consciously play the role of Judas goat. Or rather, I choose to not believe that.

But even if my belief is absolutely, always and everywhere dead right, that does not help very much. After all, the real Judas goats are not conscious of their role, and no doubt feel no need to transcend it. But they still perform that role.

Put another way, Judas goatship can be as alive and insidious when consultants are unaware of it in self or others, as when they actively despise that role. Hence, with the goal of creating a greater self-consciousness concerning how any of us might fall into a Judas goat role, I have distinguished four varieties encounterable in the world, and readers no doubt can expand that short list. It will all come to a similar point, however long or short the list. Brief descriptions of these four varieties of Judas goats may help reduce their incidence and hence contribute some to the resolution of the central question: when to proffer and when to withhold OD services?

1. Pied Pipers.   These are an attractive and even fun-loving variety of Judas goat. Their characteristic cry has some such elements. "Why not do what I do? It's fun!" This variety is well-meaning, of course, but neglectful of the differences between the positions of consultant and organization member. These differences can be so great as to cause difficulty or even danger for the organization member who begins to behave too much like the consultant.

2. Unaware collaborators.   These unwitting workers are perhaps more to be pitied than censured. Their native cunning has failed them—perhaps because of having their heads turned by admiration of their formidable helping or advising skills, perhaps because of generous fees and burgeoning bills, or whatever. Commonly, in any case, unaware collaborators have become willing but unwitting dupes in someone else's conspiracy. "Tell your bosses more about yourself," goes one call of the unaware collaborators. His client adds the silent refrain: "So we can have enough on you to fire you."

Note that unaware collaboration probably seldom appears in full-blown form from the start. Consultant may not aggressively or effectively enough probe client's intent, nor prepare client about the costs of progress. So things may start with genuine and high enthusiasm, but better soon becomes worse. In one case, an unprepared client is burnt by an employee revelation, and seeks to "get even." If consultant is not tuned into client's growing disaffection, consultant may only add to it by encouraging even deeper revelations from employees.

3. Determined even-uppers.   These are temporary cases, I judge, who often get in an ego match with clients. They get trapped into trying "to show X a thing or two" in team building, for example. Nothing awkward in that, perhaps, except when the spirit is more retribution than help. "X may be the expert in his organization setting," I heard one of them hiss one day, "but I'm the main man in team building. I know the ropes here."

The sentiments are understandable, in cases. But indulging in them can be trouble, even poison. Professional transcendence is much to be hoped for in such cases, and assiduously striven for.

4. *Misguided stimulators.* This is an easy variety of Judas goatship to fall into, but the pit can be very deep and its sides slippery in the extreme. We all like to encourage or motivate, and one thing can lead to another if we try too hard to make things happen, as contrasted with allowing them to happen.

I have in mind the charismatic intervenor who was buffaloed by one team-building participant, X. X was perceived (or, really, evaluated) by the intervenor as "recalcitrant." After awhile, the intervenor was induced to taunting X: "Tell them what you think, rabbit," or some such. "Rabbit" remained taciturn for awhile, and suddenly turned on the intervenor, decking him with a right to the mouth that sent a gusher of blood from a split lip.

So this intervenor failed essentially as he succeeded in a specific.

Tactics for such attempts at stimulation can vary in severity, but they often derive from a reasonable desire to help induce an impact, albeit a desire gone awry. The case above is not very extreme, in fact. The extreme case in point certainly goes to a certain management training effort that got into the courts a few years back. The training took place "in the pit," and its motto was: "We'll do anything to help you be a better manager, even hurt you." Training equipment included a coffin, a cross, boxing gloves and paddles (for facilitators only!), and bottled oxygen to revive those who passed out from having their breathing forcibly restrained until they "accepted" some "learning,"[1] which like as not were proposed by the trainers and derived from detectivelike background checks of the trainee. For example, the trainee might be admonished to stop drinking to excess, to lose weight, or to stop adulterous slipping around.

Notes

1. I kid you not. For chilling details, see Gene Church and Conrad D. Carnes, *The Pit: A Group Encounter Defiled* (New York: Outerbridge and Lazard, 1972).

21

Value Complementarity and Providing or Withholding Consultation

The other essay in this pair gently offers some guides as to how OD intervenors might avoid Judas goatship, or at least can recognize some of its variations, along with its primary goal of defining the term and illustrating its varieties. Its partner dwells on a single defense against becoming or being made a Judas goat, and perhaps the most subtle and yet potentially the stoutest defense. Values—the reader can substitute ''ethics,'' ''ideals,'' or a similar term and I will not complain—preoccupy this piece about how to think about avoiding Judas goatship.

Thinking is neater and less problematic than doing, of course, so this enterprise is realistically limited about its ambition, which is to suggest only one way of thinking about avoiding Judas goatship. But thought has its uses, and especially when seen as a prelude to action. The thought here intends to facilitate the later choice making, or at least to add perspective to the pursuit of effective action.

''Value complementarity'' constitutes the central thought here, and it refers to the degree of normative agreement between a client system and an OD intervenor. Roughly, value complementarity is high when the client system—major executives and their culture—has normative preferences substantially like those prescribed by OD. These OD values are broadly humanist in orientation, and emphasize trust, openness, owning, and reduced risk. Moreover, those values also can be approached via organization structures and policies or procedures consistent with trust, openness, and so on.

The concept triggers several key questions. How ''high'' need value complementarity be to encourage making a Judas goatproof contract between OD consultant and client system? And what defines the ''low'' point at which withholding services is prudent? And how to estimate ''high'' and ''low,'' that is, how to differentiate one from the other?

No one can answer such questions, but the ''value complementarity'' concept permits moving toward informed approximations to answers.

Let us begin in a typical way, by going back in time. Not so long ago—let's say the mid-1960s—the common approach to guaranteeing value complementarity was straightforward. Stranger T-Group experiences were first provided for members of a possible host organization for an OD venture, with the dual preferences being to provide such experiences to as many members as possible, and especially to as many high-status members as could be accommodated. These multiple singles would then be parachuted back into the home organization, with the goal of seeding the worksite with individuals whose value complementarity had been tested and was suitably high. At some point, this seeding would generate a "critical mass" who would then proceed to build OD values into the work culture and member behavior.

There is much to be said in favor of such a conservative approach to assessing value complementarity, even today, but the traditional approach is increasingly awkward. Three features provide context for this conclusion.

- T-Grouping is far less in vogue than it was a decade or two ago, whatever else may be said of it.
- The traditional approach implies *very* high entry costs, both in terms of prior training as well as in the degree and kind of value complementarity—in having T-Group dynamics and methods serve as prototypes for workday organizations.
- The approach requires a substantial jump from here to there—from the behavior and attitudes characteristic of most organizations to the values illustrated in T-Group dynamics. Early OD ventures emphasized creating a new social order at work, nothing less.

This list of features is kept deliberately short because, even as it is, it illustrates the awkward duality of the traditional approach. For example, the seeding model provided a substantial defense against a consultant succumbing to certain forms of Judas goatship, but it did so at the expense of mightily discouraging incremental approaches to OD values. Similarly, the approach protected organization members from disappointment and even danger, as might occur when an organization is not culturally prepared for an OD experience or when its members are encouraged to greater openness for which they are later punished because power wielders soon came to have second thoughts.

Is it possible to go much beyond the traditional approach, and with relative safety for consultant and client system? Two variations on the theme of value complementarity will suggest some venues for such initiatives.

First, take the case of an autocratic but benevolent management that has no desire for broad cultural change, but nonetheless wants to extend some low-cost benefits to its employees. Assume management's motives are at least paternalistic, and may even be narrowly instrumental in the sense of gaining some leverage to reduce the probability of now-and-again efforts to organize its employees via an NLRB certification election.

What can or should an OD consultant do in such a case? Not much could be done were the seeding model to provide guidance. But I can see sufficient (if limited) value complementarity in such cases. For example, a flexible work hours (FWH) program might well meet a trinity of modest interests: employees could gain a satisfying degree of freedom and control over their work; management would have a low-cost yet well-received program that modifies autocratic authority in real ways but clearly does not challenge traditional management controls in root-and-branch senses; and an OD consultant could meet employee and managerial needs while taking a meaningful step down a very long pathway toward the value of enhanced and responsible freedom via a standard design that requires little training and overt attitudinal change, and yet has very high success rates and great employee appeal.[1]

This first case is not an unqualified easy piece, be it noted. Thus management's track record in how they seek to retain union-free status could well be an issue; and which international or local union is the likely organizer also could be relevant. Moreover, consultant has to be scrupulously clear with management that the flexi-time installation is corrosive in basic senses of traditional notions of authority and motivation, especially if management persists in viewing FWH as only a low-cost fringe benefit. And the OD consultant always has to deal with the issue of being used only as a cooling-out agent or—to put it in more extravagant language—as a Judas goat for those in power who seek only to buy time with specific soporifics or illusory pie in the sky.

How to avoid the darker outcomes, or at least to reduce their incidence? Each consultant will have to find his own way, essentially, but some general notions do apply. For example, the consultant might well lean toward transcending the immediate intervention, which makes both strategic as well as tactical sense. In the case of FWH, consultant might well direct attention to associated processes challenged by the installation. Supervisory/employee trust is one such target, as is feedback. Even more ambitious, job redesign to create more individual or group control over the flow of work while encouraging greater involvement also would have much to recommend it. Not only does such job redesign aid and abet FWH installations by reducing the problems of assigning responsibility and measuring performance. But job redesign also increases responsible freedom at work, which serves OD values. And if nothing else, consultant could encourage some useful practices, as in action research efforts to test periodically for the effects of a FWH installation to legitimate reciprocal linkages between management and employees.

Such initiatives use the FWH installation as a beachhead for other movement toward OD goals, and use consultant's skills, while they also reduce the probability of mere Judas goatship.

Second, on numerous occasions consultant/client value complementarity might be quite limited and yet still provide several useful venues for acting on OD values. Third-party consultation,[2] role negotiation,[3] or the demotion experience[4] illustrate these *limited-purpose contracts*. Commonly, such interventions are limited—in terms of scope, time, audience, and so on—and hence fall far short of the traditional OD model of seeding for basic social change. At the same time, such interventions can be powerful vehicles for later motivation of precisely such movement, perhaps paradoxically by focusing on issues of immediate managerial relevance, and in narrow time frames.

Consider the "demotion experience," which one management gingerly accepted on consultant's recommendation as an alternative to firing a baker's dozen of sales managers. The management was sad about the firings, and had delayed them vainly well beyond the point of consensus about their unavoidability. Demotions were seen as invitations for trouble for both employee and organization, with awkward adjustments to the new status being the rule, in management's unanimous view. But demotion did provide one way around the firings, with all they implied for past and future employees. So management accepted the risk, despite their preconceptions. A design based on OD values provide broadly useful, not only for the specific issue but in downstream senses as well. In sum, management retained a batch of experienced and satisfactory performers; almost all employees accepted the demotion option rather than an attractive "golden handshake," went on to be solid performers in their new jobs, and in most cases were later promoted again; and consultant introduced an option that permitted enhanced choice making by both management and employees in confronting a dismal but unavoidable reality.

Notes

1. For an early demonstration, see Robert T. Golembiewski, Richard Hilles, and Munro Kagno, "A Longitudinal Study of Flexi-Time Effects: An OD Structural Intervention," *Journal of Applied Behavioral Science* 10 (Dec. 1974): 503–32.
2. Richard Walton, *Interpersonal Peacemaking* (Reading, Mass.: Addison-Wesley, 1969).
3. Roger Harrison, "Role Negotiation," 84–96, in W. Warner Burke and Harvey A. Hornstein, eds., *The Social Technology of Organization Development* (Washington, D.C.: NTL Learning Resources Corp., 1972).
4. Robert T. Golembiewski, Stokes B. Carrigan, Walter R. Mead, Robert Munzenrider and Arthur Blumberg, "Toward Building New Work Relationships: An Action Design for a Critical Intervention," *Journal of Applied Behavioral Science* 8 (March 1972): 135–48.

22

Toward Enhancing OD's Future

We were debriefing at the end of several long sessions on strategic planning, enjoying each other and even the overpriced opulence around us, when the talk turned serious. Does OD have a future? That became the topic that carried us through dinner and its aftermath of cordials. It became increasingly clear the *the* question really was: Do *we* have a future, as representatives of a collective and vibrant consciousness, doing what we value so highly?

The setting was appropriate. We were all ODers in Southern California's Orange County. Newness and squeaky cleanness dominated. Certainly the past almost dared not intrude there. Where did they keep their junk cars? Even fallen leaves did not seem tolerated lest, I suppose, they create even tiny doubts about the permanence of perfection. In any case, one had to search for fallen leaves around our lush home away from home. The future tense also directly suited our work of the past few days. We had been looking ahead, hard, for an organization whose twists and turns would influence many, and we were in effect influencing that portentious future.

So the special appropriateness, there, of two questions. Does OD have a future? Do we have a future?

Answers are not easy to come by, and at best the caveats dominate. So I have to hedge in giving this answer: Well, yes, of course. But things could go very wrong. This hedge serves constructive purposes, and it also provides conservative context for five interlocking and reinforcing factors that will contribute to an affirmative answer. The absence of these factors, or lesser emphases on them, will encourage a negative outcome. In sum: Well, yes; and then, maybe no.

Note that I write here of the future in connection only with the several institutional embodiments of OD—the OD Network, the various competence-enhancing programs of NTL and University Associates, the several university programs leading to a Master's degree in OD, and so on. Note also that I believe the bundle of values and activities called OD will continue to be applied, and moreso by increasing numbers of specialists and line managers, whatever happens to OD's present outward signs of its inward grace-cum-technology.

117

1. OD will have an institutional future to the degree that it encompasses—effectively as well as firmly—policy and structural interventions. Of course, it will continue to include the interaction-centered emphases that today define so much of OD's content for so many. The issue revolves less about where to start than about what constitutes a reasonably coherent view of where to stop. The common failure to emphasize reinforcement—of interaction reinforced by policy and structural changes, or vice versa—is the culprit. As OD practitioners resist such mutuality, so also will the momentum of the movement be arrested, and so also will pieces of the institutional cultural core be eroded and chipped off—by QWL, by HRD, Organization Transformation, or whatever.

In effect, any strong emphasis on interaction inclines OD to the always present. But organizations are rooted in the policies and structures developed in the past, and these—*unless uprooted or modified*—will powerfully influence attitudes and behaviors in the future. Hence OD will have to broaden its central vision to provide coequal status for structure as well as policies and procedures, or it will diminish—no ifs, ands, or buts.

More pointedly, OD *should* diminish, failing in that inclusion. If OD values and culture cannot guide or discipline policies and structures within a professional area of study and application, one can hardly be sanguine about the likelihood that this will occur within organizations.

2. OD will have an institutional future to the degree that valid and reliable means are developed to improve quality control of what gets done, and how. This involves not only providing some review of current practices, but perhaps moreso requires the cultivation of a passion for continuing renewal and improvement in the shared standards by which practice will be judged, and to which levels of aspiration will be pegged.

Hope should be nourished, but the experience in NTL and then CCI suggests that this QC effort will not be an easy piece. See also "A Statement of Values and Ethics. . . ."

3. OD will have an institutional future, relatedly, to the degree that its adherents have organizational and substantive roots for their orientation and technology. What constitute "roots"? Generally, I refer to functional or policy specializations to which OD values and skills can be wedded. In academia, this means that many OD intervenors will have firm roots in the traditional disciplines—Sociology, Psychology, and so on. For internal intervenors, this means that more and more of them will be "Comp and Benefits" people with OD skills and orientations, or industrial relations folk who operate in OD modes, and so on and on. These polyspecialists contrast with OD as "staff" personnel.

I am inspired to doggerel, and purloined at that:

> OD without policies and
> structures has no roots;

> Lacking OD values and supporting
> interaction, structures and
> policies can have strange fruits.

In general opposition, ODers today tend to be viewed as, and also *tend to be*, disembodied from such functional or disciplinary contexts. ODers tend to be generalists in the quicksilveredness of interaction, and this has serious long-run costs as well as some immediate conveniences. Thus there is the facilitative-only trap, which often is augmented by a kind of vestal virgin role—ODers as those outside the go-go of the organization who are called only to help clean up afterwards, rather than being involved in preventative efforts. The prime consequences of this restricted role generate these awkwardnesses, and more:

- OD values and orientations do not get reflected in the design of congenial structures and reward systems, but get inclined toward Band-Aid models after inhospitable institutions generate the awkward effects they often do.
- ODers may feel "used" and put in cooling-out roles
- Interaction-dominant ODers heighten the risks of personal burnout and emotional exhaustion, which can be moderated by the task rotation and cross-training required by the "roots" approach prescribed here
- OD units are targets of envy and anger as not "carrying their weight in what really matters."

There are many variations on the present theme of substantive "roots" for OD, one important illustration of which refers to the moderation of the organization politics often triggered by OD success. As OD prospers in an organization, so also are bodies and dollars added to explicitly OD budgets, and these additions to "overhead" become increasingly attractive targets for raiding by line officials, especially when times get rough, as they periodically will. Something like this scenario occurred at Corning Glass, in the U.S. Army, and at SmithKline Corp., for example. The "roots" approach distributes OD bodies/dollars in the several budgets of functional units, in contrast, typically with greater power than OD units. The trick here is sufficient networking for these organizationally dispersed OD resources to achieve sufficient critical masses appropriate to variable situational demands.

4. OD will have an institutional future to the degree that it gives telling attention to developing longer and more explicit "career chains" for internal consultants.

For internal OD consultants, the traditional hierarchical chains are short, and ought to be. That is, longer traditional chains in OD units in a few organizations have been developed but only at severe cost—charges of empire building, which invites longer-run retribution by organizational others. Hence the inappropriateness of traditional approaches—indeed, their danger—and hence the special need to develop places for internal ODers to go. The prescription above to focus on functional "roots" with OD perspectives helps address this need, lest OD jobs be seen as a revolving door for short-timers, or deadends for long-time employees. Both of these alternatives have serious implications for the persistence of institutional expressions of OD.

Each organization will tend toward uniqueness in how this problem is solved, but one generic solution seems obvious. ODers often recommend cross-training as a convenient solution to many organizational problems, and the present view only prescribes that they take some of their own medicine. The U.S. Army illustrates an extreme approach. All potential ODers had to have prior records of command success, as well as high rank—typically captain or major. They would then be trained in OD, with all knowing they "had been there," which all but guaranteed their credibility. After a tour or two, these ODers would return to line jobs.

This prescription has serious implications. For example, it discourages programs like a "Master of Arts in OD," *unless* the specialization (OD) is balanced by a corresponding concentration in a policy or arena specialization (e.g., in strategic planning, compensation and benefits, budgeting and finance, collective bargaining, and so on and on). As is generally the case, narrow training invites a restricted vision, as well as a heightened vulnerability to the shifting fashions and emphases that characterize organizational life. Even the healthiest dinosaurs had problems when the environment changed!

5. OD will have an institutional future to the degree that it pays attention to its past. This involves honoring its posterity, while transcending the people and the products that constitute that prosperity.

A following essay—"Does OD Sufficiently Honor Its Past?"—will provide detail concerning this fifth point in a highly selective evocation of how the odds in favor of OD's institutionalized persistence can be enhanced.

23

Toward a Contingency View of Certification: Professionalism, Performance, and Protectionism

Professionalization is perhaps the most common prescription for what ails our organizational society, in both public and business sectors, for purposes both deadly earnest and otherwise. Let the reader judge the recent Canadian enthusiasm for professionalizing streetwalkers and ecdysiasts.

No wonder, then, that professionalization and certification have attracted the attention of many in OD. Some like them, and some do not.

This seems like an appropriate balance, because the case for professional certification leading to more or better performance is neither clear nor consistent.[1] This present contingency analysis seeks to prescribe some of the conditions that will influence if not determine a critical balance—that between performance <---> protectionism. Since both of these will follow in the wake of growing professionalization, one need not ask: Professionalization—yes or no? Rather the key question involves: How much of which effects of professionalization?

Hence the organization of what follows. Immediately, the first section seeks to describe the general case for professionalization's contribution to performance. In turn, separate sections will then focus on factors that will shift the practical balance—toward performance, or toward protectionism.

The Case for Professionalization <---> Performance

The ideal of professionalization can be associated with enhanced performance, and the argument has a potent quality. Professionalization in its idealized form reflects the development of an increasingly targeted sense of good and prudent practices, as well as of institutions for motivating and enforcing that development. No wonder, then, that public confidence and trust lead to increasing grants of status and autonomy to the "real professionals."

In practice, of course, substantial reservations might be appropriate about the closeness of the linkage between professionalization and performance. Professionalization also can foster protectionism as well as performance. For example, a profession might erect barriers to the entry of deserving outsiders while reducing innovation or competition by insiders.

What factors influence, if not determine, this critical balance between protectionism and performance? The two following sections provide perspective on this central question.

Features Encouraging Performance

Five examples suggest the reach and scope of a full list of ways in which professionalization contributes to performance.

1. A passion for continuous testing.   Perhaps primarily, performance will be served by continuous testing and improvements in a body of theory and guides for action that, in combination with ethically based codes of "good practices," permit reasonable judgments concerning "prudent practices." This is the heart of the claim of professionals—that they encompass sufficient knowledge for prescribing with substantial precision what a professional should do under various circumstances.

Professions should be dynamic rather than static, however, so the process sketched above is problem as well as solution. Once a model of good practices is established, for example, major forces can reinforce persistence even in the face of substantial evidence to the contrary. These forces derive from self-interest, the arcane processes of diffusing innovations, and myriad other sources. For example, the Flexner report[2] concerning medical practices saw the triumph of a germ-specific theory of disease, which supplanted only with time and great effort the cavalier conventions of an earlier day. Major contributions though they were, the Flexnerian advances were also barriers to the later extension of medical practices to encompass environmental contributions to disease. The implications are profound. Consider only the radically different emphases on, and approaches to, preventative medicine implied by germ-specific versus environmental models of disease when it comes to cancer research and prevention.

2. A commitment to continuous renewal.   Since every model of "good practices" probably will constitute an advance today as well as a barrier to useful change tomorrow, a vital sense of continuous renewal must suffuse any profession. Hence the need for periodic Flexner reports in every profession, in effect.

3. A deep concern with standards for practice.   A healthy professionalization will reflect a reasonable and enforceable set of standards for circumscribing good and prudent practices. The development of an accepted and enforceable code of ethics constitutes one aspect of this critical activity, which essentially rests on some viable institutions and traditions for enforcement. Enforcement can cover a broad range—from peer review to direct regulation by government agencies.[3]

4. Career-long learning for professionals.   Relatedly, professionalization with a dominant thrust toward performance will emphasize meaningful continuing education. Enough said, but implementation is another matter.

5. A receptivity to external review.   A professionalization inclined toward performance also will be receptive to external review, or at least tolerant of it. In its several forms, external review can help reinforce and support the public sense of confidence and trust that constitutes the heart of professionalization.

The form of external review is far less critical than the openness to it, in general. Setting aside those cases in which external review is for appearances only, provision for external scrutiny implies a commitment that can facilitate continual renewal and increase the broad sense of trust and confidence underlying the public grant of autonomy and status to professions. Resistance to external review suggests, even if it clearly does not establish, a closedness that would encourage protectionism over the longer run.

Typically, professions resist such external review, as in the caustic smugness that asks: What can they tell us about how we do our work? Such a view might be useful in the early stages of professionalization, but it is longer-run poison.

Features Encouraging Protectionism

The impetus of professionalization toward heightened performance will be blunted by numerous and powerful forces at the very heart of what it means to be "professional." As Larson reminds us, professionalization involves a dual process—that by which the producers of a special service not only seek to create a market for their services but also strive to control that market for their expertise.[4] Moreover, not only do professionals have derivative and patent economic motives, but these are reinforced by a special social status that can clothe such motives in righteous rationales.

Hence expectations about the effects of professionalization must be realistically balanced, in the best of cases.

What expectations about professionalization are better *not* entertained? The present catalog of three is illustrative only, but it does suggest the broader range of what professionalization should not be expected to do. The negative form is used in all cases to reinforce the position that the expectations should be avoided, or at least subjected to careful scrutiny before being embraced.

1. Not clearly the tide of the future.   In many accounts, one gets the sense that professionalization is a kind of inexorable historical imperative, so appropriate that it sweeps all before it. In this view, ODers need only acknowledge the inevitable to solve their major problems by defining themselves as professionals.[5]

In point of fact, deference to and trust of professionals is at least being seriously challenged, and indeed today's tide may be running the opposite way.[6]

Some observers see these crosscurrents as characteristic of developed societies,[7] and no one seems to seriously challenge the position that crosscurrents exist in medicine, education, and a broad range of traditional professional services.[8]

Which is stronger: the trend toward or against professionalization? Observers differ. Bell sees the antiforces as stronger,[9] while Haug[10] and others take the opposite point of view.

The major point is that conventional professional practices seem to cut in several ways. The crosscurrents sketched above consequently should be fully valued in estimates of the performance <--> protectionism balance likely to result from even energetic and well-intentioned efforts toward professionalization in OD.

2. Not obviously a house in order. Professionalization implies such an attractive image—heightened neatness, precision, and standards of public-spirited and compassionate service—that it can encourage neglect of various untidy realities. Rest assured that the attainment of professional status will not resolve troublesome realities. Certainly, preaching about professional status will not.

OD has its share of troublesome realities, and their management is probably better seen, on balance, as a prelude to certification rather than a consequence of it. See "A Rose by any Other Name?," "Is QWL OD's Charge?," and so on.

The spuriousness of the comfy illusion is perhaps best investigated at higher levels of magnification, as it were. Indeed, rather than professionalization representing a house in order, even the established professions like medicine and law seem to need major and periodic assessments of the relationships between practitioners and clients.[11] The full catalog of supporting particulars cannot be presented here, but a few illustrations should suggest that OD has more to do than to "be like" the established professions. Illustratively, even established professions face such challenges:

- Professional autonomy may rest on monopoly control as much as, or even more than, on knowledge.[12]
- Various aspects of professions-in-action—ideologies, interaction with clients, and so on—reflect a need for power and status as much as, or even more than, optimal approaches to helping clients.[13]
- Evidence about the efficiency and effectiveness of professionals is often poor and inconclusive.[14]
- Evidence implies that professional self-discipline and self-control are often inadequate, even chronically so.[15]

Extreme conclusions will not be drawn from such evidence. Although "being professional" may have an attractive ring, issues like the ones illustrated above do not succumb to verbalisms. The balance in OD will be moved toward performance only grudgingly and with great effort, at least at times, to judge from the experience of the established professions.

3. Not free of contradictory tensions.   Arguments for professionalization in OD often emphasize the rosy side of things—the enhancement of performance, the publicly spirited provision of expert services by the autonomous and self-directing practitioner, and so on.

But these common arguments underweigh some contradictory and self-canceling tendencies of professionalization. Consider only the basic issue of professionals in bureaucracies. Much commentary proposes that bureaucracy undercuts professions;[16] and some have also made the counterargument that professions will (or could, or should) induce substantial modifications in bureaucratic practices.[17] Thus bureaucracies emphasize hierarchy, and their associated culture often values local loyalty and substantial dependence of members. These features contrast sharply with "the professional": guided by a code of ethics that reflects universal rather than organizational standards, collegiality rather than hierarchy, commitment and loyalty to their profession as distinguished from their employing organization, self-discipline and autonomy rather than hierarchical control, and so on.

This is not the place to foretell how these complex contradictory tendencies will work themselves out in bureaucracies. But the clash will be substantial, and in cases even momentous. And it is not at all clear what the specific balance will be between performance and protectionism, at specific points in time. Hence the appropriateness of such defenses as that proposed in "A Fund for Displaced ODers."

Conclusion

In sum, striving toward professionalization in OD has powerful motivators, but major tethers on enthusiasm exist. These boundary conditions fall in two classes. They involve emphasis on what can be done to tilt professionalization toward enhanced performance; and these conditions also require restraining expectations about what professionalization can do and under which conditions. Ironically, expansive expectations are likely to encourage a kind of professionalization that inclines more toward protectionism than performance.

Notes

1. For a balanced view of professionalism's features and effects, see Margli S. Larson, *The Rise of Professionalism* (Berkeley: University of California, 1977).
2. Abraham Flexner, *Medical Education in the United States and Canada.* Bulletin Number 4, Carnegie Foundation for the Advancement of Teaching, 1910.

3. For an overview of the range of possible enforcement modes, see Robert D. Blair and Stephen Rubin, eds., *Regulating the Professions* (Lexington, Mass.: D.C. Heath, 1980).

4. Larson, *The Rise of Professionalism*.

5. Harold L. Wilensky, "The Professionalization of Everyone?" *American Journal of Sociology* 70 (1964): 137–58.

6. Helena Z. Lopata, "Expertization of Everyone and the Revolt of the Client," *Sociological Quarterly* 17 (Autumn 1976): 435–47.

7. Daniel Bell, *The Coming of Post-Industrial Society* (New York: Basic Books, 1973).

8. Lopata, "Expertization;" James A. Belasco, Joseph A. Alutto, and Alan Glassman, "A Case Study of Community and Teacher Expectations Concerning the Authority Structure of School Systems," *Education and Urban Society* 4 (Nov. 1971): 85–97; and others.

9. Bell, *Post-Industrial Society*.

10. Marie R. Haug, "The Deprofessionalization of Everyone?" *Sociological Focus* 8 (Aug. 1975): 197–213.

11. Brenda Danet, "Client-Organization Relationships," 384–85, in Paul C. Nystrom and William H. Starbuck, eds., *Handbook of Organizational Design* (New York: Oxford University Press, 1981).

12. Haug, *Deprofessionalization*, and Larson, *The Rise of Professionalism*.

13. Joseph R. Gusfield, *Illusions of Authority* (Chicago: University of Chicago Press, 1980).

14. E.g., Allen E. Bergin, "The Evaluation of Therapeutic Outcomes," 217–70 in Allen E. Bergin and Sol L. Garfield, eds., *Handbook of Psychotherapy and Behavior Change* (New York: Wiley, 1971).

15. E.g., Larson, *Rise of Professionalism*.

16. Danet, Client-Organization, 393–94.

17. E.g., Peter F. Drucker, *The Age of Discontinuity* (New York: Harper & Row, 1969), esp., 264–78.

24

Toward OD Certification: "It's Not My Dog, Mister"

You may remember Jerry Harvey's shaggy-dog story that features a shaggy dog. You may know how the story went, but a brief recap will do no harm. A man walking along a seaside beach saw at a distance what seemed to be two minor sandstorms. On coming closer, he saw two holes being dug, with sand flying from already substantial excavations, located side by side. At a still closer range, our beachwalker saw two subjects hard at work. A man occupied one of the deepening holes; and in the other, of course, was a shaggy dog. Although doing pretty much the same thing, side by side, neither man nor dog paid the slightest attention to the other.

The beachwalker was bemused. A single subject expending such furious energy in this way would have heightened anyone's interest. But two sand-shovelers—side by side, one man and one dog—induced a very powerful curiosity in the observer.

So the beachwalker asked—of the man, reasonably enough: "What's your dog doing?"

Without missing a motion, although already bathed in sweat, the human sand-shoveler replied: "It's not my dog, mister." The human shoveler did not even look up, leaving our nonplussed beachwalker to form his own conclusions.

No record of the dog's view is available.

I have forgotten what point, if any, Harvey made with his unlikely duo of diggers in the sand. But it strikes me that the basic symbol and its implied lesson both relate to OD practitioners, and especially concerning the issue of certification and its conceptual baggage: the development of entrance qualifications to improve the breed, periodic reviews to both encourage and assess that OD practitioners do not "die on the vine" after an initial certification or two, and (among many other features) a code of ethics for practice which provides guidance for practice and which in a few extreme cases can be utilized to deny practitioners their legitimating license.

How is the human sand-shoveler like OD practitioners? That's easy enough an image to transfer. Two consultants might be working side by side in an organization, doing what appear to the casual watcher to be more or less the same things. To simplify matters, assume that one person is clearly labeled an "OD practitioner," but the label of the other is not clear. So the interested watcher asks: "What's the other person doing, and how well?" And the response from OD practitioners has tended to be: "It's not my business, sister (or mister)."

This is an awkward position for the OD practitioner, for compelling reasons. Paramountly, perhaps, what some are doing may be associated by others quite directly with one's business, and especially if they are doing "it" artlessly or in disregard of definitions of what constitutes today's reasonable praxis. One's "OD" may be tarred and feathered appropriate to someone else's misguided practice, in short. This is particularly the case when "OD by razor blade" is practiced, as has been known to happen. You know how that one goes. The glass door read "Management Consultant." Then comes the razor blade, and after a few strokes of the paintbrush—*voila!*—the legend now reads "Organization Development."

How one looks at the person digging that other hole also affects one's response. "They are just trying to make a buck while serving a purpose" encourages the usual response, as does a lack of interest about who is digging which holes and about what holes are being dug. Try another perspective on for size: "They are fouling a water hole." If you see OD as life sustaining—as a kind of special and rare source for refreshing organizations as well as the people in them—you are more likely to take the second perspective than the first.

"It's not my dog" may have been a reasonable response at one time, of course. In earlier days, for example, the issue was more one of encouraging people to join in than it was differentiating the character and quality of those joining in. Moreover, far less clarity once existed about what qualified as "acceptable practice," given what was then known or reasonably suspected. This would encourage humility about quality control, obviously.

Then was then, however, and now is now. Moreover, one must always guard against the protectionist aspects of accredition, concerns about which no doubt encourage responses like: "It's not my dog, mister." Keeping the other guy out can be personally profitable at some times, but it can also deprive an area of testing and hence growth. See also the preceding essay: "Professionalization, Performance, and Protectionism: A Contingency View."

Even when discounted by such factors, the common position about accreditation today is awkward, if not self-defeating or even suicidal.

The challenge is clear, then: can specialists in the continuous renewal of everyone else's organizations take their own medicine? Equally clearly, credibility can come only from accepting and then conquering this challenge, and not from seeking to avoid it by taking a permissive attitude toward what others are doing in the name of OD.

Given this awkwardness, if not worse, of the "common position about accreditation," could the present view be mistaken about who has done what and how often? Perhaps. But even a thumbnail history should establish the essential accuracy of the present characterization of the usual response to accreditation. Note that this history relates to four institutions central in OD's history and to a fifth that may play a major future role but in any case is off to a great start. The oldies include: National Training Laboratories, or NTL; International Association of Applied Social Scientists, or IAASS, then Certified Consultants International, or CCI, and now defunct; the OD Network or ODN; and the Organization Development Institute, or OD Institute. The Human Systems Development Consortium is the very promising latecomer.

NTL began selecting "network members" beginning in the late 1950s, and still does so. But that venerable body shrank from certification, noting a basic conflict of interest in the NTL's basic mission as program-provider. The associated practical exigencies patently could make it awkward to also serve as certifier of practitioners. Or at least NTL would be vulnerable to the charge of serving its practical interests if it also made certification decisions.

IAASS, later CCI, sought to fill the certification breech, with NTL support. CCI members did develop a certification process and elaborated a regional structure for peer reviews, but at its most expansive CCI achieved only a few hundred members. Today is not its best day, despite efforts to link up with various other professional groups—a useful effort headed-up by Herb Shepard, whose death in August 1985 cut him off in the fullness of his powers but hopefully will inspire concerted energies by others to complete what he began. CCI recently went out of business.

There is plenty to do, for certain, as is suggested by the size of the OD Network's membership. It numbers in the mid-thousands, and contrasts sharply with a CCI membership never higher than the mid-hundreds. But ODN is definitely not in the certification business, and resists any such overtures. It provides identification, support, fun, and professional development, in about that order.

The Organization Development Institute, still nurtured basically by Don Cole after all these years, provides growing hope that the needed things related to certification will get done. OD Institute has a membership far smaller than ODN's. But OD Institute has always required a review for those seeking membership and, far more important, its founder and guiding spirit has succeeded in aiding the development of a comprehensive code of ethics. A phased process has been decided on—wisely, in my view. 1985 constituted the first year of developing understanding about the standards of the code, so as to build the commitment that can later support reliance on the code for quality-control purposes. (See also "A Statement of Values and Ethics . . .").

The Statement constitutes perhaps the most positive reflection of movement toward productive certification. The phases approach has much to recommend it, but perhaps more important is the history of the progressive institutionalization of the Human Systems Development Consortium, or HSDC, which is basically responsible for generating the Statement. HSDC began within the Center for the Study of Ethics in the Professions at the Illinois Institute of Technology, with co-project directors Mark S. Frankel and William Gellerman. The project developed collaborative relations with a covey of OD and human systems development associations, some of which had a history of differences. The project then succeeded in attracting a grant from the National Science Foundation, and in the summer of 1986 the project transferred to the American Association for the Advancement of Science.

HSDC has generated several useful products, and promises more. Their "A Statement of Values and Ethics" will be considered in Part III, and a useful annotated bibliography has been published quite recently.[1]

So the history is clear enough. Mostly, in effect, OD users have said about the certification of others: "It's not my dog, mister." But real hope seems justified that a greater sense of professional responsibility for what is going on not only still exists but is gaining momentum. The issue is far from settled but, as I say, real hope does not appear Pollyannaish.

Note

1. Mark S. Frankel, ed. *Values and Ethics in Organization and Human Systems Development: An Annotated Bibliography* (Washington, D.C.: American Association for the Advancement of Science, Office of Scientific Freedom and Responsibility, October 1987).

25

Toward a National Institute of Planned and Peaceful Change: Visioning about Our Future

A lot of music lovers have heard the one about Tchaikovsky. The dialog goes something like this:

Question: How many symphonies did Tchaikovsky write?

Answer: The Fourth, Fifth, and Sixth symphonies.

There is more truth than poetry to this one. People tend to remember you—indeed, perhaps *should* remember you—for what you did at your peak. Hence Tchaikovsky's phantom first three symphonies. They are little remembered, and may deserve to be, for all I know. (I am not absolutely tone deaf, but I do respond most affirmatively to a single note—that of the dinner bell.) In any case, aficionados apparently start counting with Tchaikovsky's Fourth Symphony.

The general question may be put to OD. What might OD accomplish at its peak? Or put otherwise, what is the best product by which it would most like to be known?

These are institutional versions of the same kind of forbidding question that is part of so many career-planning designs. What would you want to have said of you on your tombstone, or in your obituary?

Since I have the temerity in this case to write about institutional objectives for OD, it is only fair to provide the reader with a hint—I trust it is "the sense"—of my personal objectives. What goes on that tombstone? More than once, I have thought about it, hard. And when push comes to shove, when all the relevant things are said and evaluated, that legend comes down to this bottom line:

> Like all people, he had his price; but few people bid high enough to learn what it was.

The precedent for brevity having been set at the personal level, I contrive to be even more parsimonious at the institutional level. By what product might OD be best known? Let me say it directly: by the development of a National Institute of Planned and Peaceful Change (NIPPC).

Now I could stop right at this point, but brevity can be overdone! Immediately, several caveats are in order. Due apologies must go, of course, to the National Institutes of Health. NIH provides a useful model for such a NIPPC, and the focus on change is hardly new. Thus the American Arbitration Association—an eventual component of NIPPC?—has been acting on one variety of nonviolent change for quite a time. Moreover, today is hardly the most politically opportune time to take up the cudgels for NIPPC, or anything like it.

But caveats do not carry the day. We usually have time to do things over and over, to cite one positive motivator, so maybe some day—even this day!—enough people may come to the conclusion that it is worth taking the time to do appropriate things the first time around. Moreover, some ideas are good enough that they bear repeating, lest their usefulness be forgotten.

So what might be the form and substance for NIPPC? This is neither the appropriate time nor occasion for fine detail, but some broadbrush strokes may be helpful.

Broadly, a matrix design might perhaps best typify a reasonable structure for NIPPC. At least three facets of such a matrix come to mind:

- a facet dealing with the levels of organization at which peaceful and planned change might be waged: individuals, pairs, small groups, groups of groups, and so on.
- a facet dealing with the available classes of designs which might be utilized, generally, to induce change via attention to behaviors and attitudes, policies and procedures, or structures for relating people.
- a facet dealing with the temporal modes of intervention, which would include at least: preventive or anticipatory interventions; immediately reactive or soon-after-the-fact interventions, as in ameliorative efforts after some natural or manmade calamity, in arbitration, or negotiation; and perhaps long-after-the-fact interventions, which utilize historigraphical, biographical, or ethnological methods to analyze past events so as to shed light on current or anticipated events.

These facets might be represented in various ways, the simplest of which is the cube depicted below in Figure 25.1. Even this highly simplified cube has 6 × 3 × 3, or 54 cells, which suggest the richness of targeted detail that might be encompassed by a NIPPC.

Such a relative goliath might be considered an anachronism in this day of "smaller is better," but then again it can be cogently argued that NIPPC is but an inexpensive step toward doing what needs to be done, with all-around savings for most actors as well as for their social systems. For example, I have conducted an informal poll among managers and executives over the last decade or so, and I have several thousand estimates of the time that organization leaders attribute to conflict resolution.

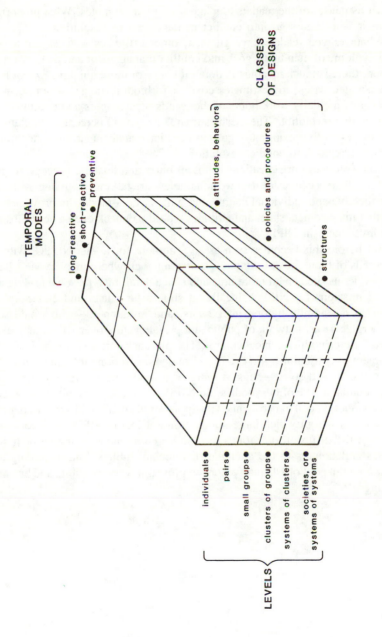

Figure 25.1   A Matrix of Targets for a National Institute of Planned and Peaceful Change.

Let us pause for the readers to make their own estimates. What proportion of their work hours go into conflict management or resolution?

Whatever you readers have guessed, other estimates suggest that a very large volume of man hours goes into conflict management and that, by implication, there is much leverage in doing it better or more quickly. Except for a few isolated cases, my estimates cover a forbidding range—from 20 to 75 percent of the daily work hours of thousands of managers and executives go into conflict resolution. The mean estimate? Nearly 40 percent of all managerial and executive man hours go into conflict management and—hopefully, but not likely—into conflict resolution.

Now conflict in organizations is not all burrs and thistles, I recognize, and useful catharsis can result. But we nonetheless are talking about huge volumes of collective and individual energy and will. Even a modest improvement in conflict management skills and attitudes would pay back even a very substantial investment in NIPPC.

But before this becomes seen as an argument for a vast NIPPC, with its hundreds of thousands of minnions scurrying everywhere in everyone's businesses, let us spend a bit more time and space detailing a reasonable style and set of missions for NIPPC. Ideally, it should be a lean and elite corps of stimulators—administrators, intervenors, and researchers—who would seek to energize a vast network of public and private actors over whom they exercised little or no hierarchical control. The outreach activities of the U.S. Department of Agriculture—in extension, in demonstration plots, in diffusion of innovations, and so on—suggest more of a model in this regard than some overpopulated hive of busybodies. So NIPPC would help mobilize resources, and conduct crucial experiments with applications that could serve as demonstration sites from which large numbers might learn. NIPPC also could encourage the diffusion of various techniques-cum-values, bringing both successes and failures to the attention of relevant publics, and upgrading and enlarging the pool of OD intervenors employed in various public and business settings.

Part III

PERSPECTIVES ON MOVING FROM HERE TO THERE

Introduction

Doubtless, it remains a very long distance from "where OD is" to what "OD might become." Hence the centrality of this third and final part of *Ideas and Issues*, which provides some reasonable next steps for moving "from here to there." Lacking such convenient next steps, OD might become so enamored of the ideal as to become lost in today's hurly-burly.

Part III contains nine thought pieces, or interpretive vignettes, that help provide short-run guidance for OD. All such divisions are variously artificial, but these nine pieces may be conveniently thought of as dealing with three general themes:

- protecting what might be called the "OD core" (selections 26 through 29;
- dealing with certain topics that illustrate OD's reach and grasp (selections 30 through 32); and
- helping orient the personal performance of those persons in OD roles (selections 33 and 34).

1. Protecting the "OD core": selections 26 through 29. Getting from here to any there for OD will require protecting and enhancing what may be called its "core," perhaps first and foremost. If that defining "core" is either lost or given insufficient care and attention, it will be of no consequence that OD survives as a "shell" or an empty label. Four selections indicate what is meant in specific terms by this elemental consideration.

A significant part of protecting OD's core involves being clear on the values defining caring and competent practice, and that issue is much in the air nowadays. " 'A Statement of Values and Ethics . . . ,'" to begin, directs attention to a signal recent development among those dealing with human systems. After many revisions over the years, a code for ODers is being circulated widely to solicit reactions that may require yet another round of revision. But the prime purpose has moved beyond the formative and into an educative phase—to showcase the Statement as a way of educating the several communities of researchers and intervenors concerned with human systems development. This is a step toward some kind of formal status for the Statement, which over the longer-run might even support some program of certification. Guidelines for practice, of course, constitute one of the prerequisites for a profession.

How OD is merchandized, patently, also will have an impact on the degree to which its core is protected. Hence the significance of "Not Whether to Market, but What." In marketing terms, that is, the selection focuses on Krell's suggestion that OD may be a "maturing" product line. This is to say that OD may be in serious trouble. For the businesslike approach to maturing products is to "milk" them, to skimp on research and development, and to emphasize spurious differentiation among similar products, among other awkwardnesses. All these are terminal preliminaries to the product dying, as it were.

The second selection below urges attention to the "what" of OD, then, as contrasted to marketing processes per se. Specifically, the selection reminds us, OD reflects a commitment to a set of humanistic values, places basic reliance on process analysis, and emphasizes organizational structures and procedures appropriate for growthful human relationships. Marketing OD, as "packaged" in these three ways, presents no great problems. Marketing OD without reference to these three essentials saves the shell by jeopardizing the core.

Protecting OD's core also involves a specific orientation to its posterity, or so the argument goes in "Does OD Sufficiently Honor Its Past?" That specific orientation involves two simultaneous postures, as it were—caring enough about OD progenitors to honor them, while being prepared to build on their achievements while acknowledging and transcending their limitations.

The third selection dwells on a nagging suspicion that things could be far better in OD with regard to honoring its past so as to build beyond it. Indeed, so rapid has been the growth of OD, and so variegated have been the backgrounds of ODers, that the basic problem may be more the difficulty of recognizing that posterity, as contrasted with honoring it. Why this has come to be, and especially what can be done to rectify matters, get prime attention in the third selection of Part III—"Does OD Sufficiently Honor Its Past?" Earlier selections also provide perspectives on this point. The reader might review such selections in Part I as "Some Differences between OD Generations," I and II.

As a final emphasis with regard to OD's core, "The Fund for Displaced ODers" provides practical counterpoint. It is all well and good for ODers to protect their core—as in respecting the Statement of Values and Ethics, in marketing OD so as to emphasize its distinctive content, and in recognizing and honoring their posterity. But what if an ODer gets punished, in effect, for such good works?

The case is far from hypothetical, as the several discussions at professional meetings of the Statement confirm. A client may encourage—or even order—an ODer to do something in violation of the Statement, or to risk losing a client or a job. Then what? "A Fund for Displaced ODers" suggests one way of dealing with such a problem. However, the emphasis is less on a particular tactic than on the underlying conviction—that a line of praxis that fails to give serious attention to supporting its own when they are doing correct things is in deep trouble. The only similarly deep trouble will be encountered when an area of practice protects its own when they are doing mischief or, worse still, patent evil.

2. *Extending OD's reach-and-grasp: selections 30 through 32.* OD's movement from today's "here" to the "there" of the several tomorrows also will be facilitated by ODers demonstrating that "their thing" is variously central to important topics in the air. Only three examples are provided below, but the range of possibilities is substantial and the leverage they permit can be great.

"What *In Search of Excellence* Still Needs to Seek, and How OD Can Help" leads off our short list of how OD can establish its connections to important issues. Few people will need reminding that *In Search of Excellence* has been *the* blockbuster book in the management literature of this era—and of all other eras, in fact. Sales number in the millions, and the end seems nowhere in sight. Hence it may seem presumptuous of the selection below to instruct this blockbuster of a volume. But try another way to look at the matter. If OD can credibly help *In Search* in the required further seeking, so much the better for OD. In any case, the selection attempts to show what OD can add to even that book, which some see as a kind of managerial be-all and end-all. Oppositely, an OD orientation suggests that *In Search of Excellence* in basic ways points us in the wrong direction, or at least a perilous one.

OD practice deals every day with another hot topic, which constitutes the message of "Some Unintended Consequences of Intervening 'Where the Pain Is.' " Related advice appears in many forms in numerous arenas. ODers themselves are fond of noting: No pain, no gain. But it is not always clear whether that advice applies prospectively, retrospectively, or at both times.

That is, is prior pain necessary to motivate initial learning? Or is all learning painful? Or both of the above?

Similarly, observers of economic development often note that things have to hit rock bottom before pleas for renewal get taken seriously. And major debate among Poland's Solidarity members involves guessing which degree of pain—merely enormous or truly catastrophic—will be required to encourage reform of their economic and political systems.

Such congruent advice clearly deserves real attention, for there can be too much of even the very best of things. Consequently, "Some Unintended Consequences . . ." questions the generally useful prescription to intervene where the pain is felt and where, by hypothesis, major motivational energies may be engaged.

The final selection relates to demonstrating OD's reach-and-grasp. " 'Promise Not to Tell': A Critical View of 'Confidentiality' in Consultation" deals with a ubiqitous concern. Such a "promise" has a broad applicability—in the religious confessional, between lawyers, doctors, or other professionals and their clients, between friends, and so on. And "confidentiality" also is a central issue in much OD consultancy.

"Promise Not to Tell" deals with the several trade-offs inherent in confidentiality, and goes beyond them to sketch this consultant's personal approach to the issues involved. That is, "confidentiality" can make available critical information enhancing both the well-being of the client as well as the competence of the consultant. That is the good news. At the same time, however, "confidentiality" can bind and restrict as well as facilitate. "Promise" seeks a personally workable resolution of these forces in opposition.

3. Orientating the OD practitioner: selections 33 and 34. Two final selections have a distinctly personal thrust. They seek to highlight some common choices and dilemmas facing OD intervenors, both as people and as professionals.

"The OD Intervenor: Wonder Woman/Superman, or On-Call Facilitator?" attempts to deal with the central issue of how intervenors define self and their competence or potency. Where to draw the line, as in the basic judgment about "making it happen" versus "allowing it to happen"? The latter role is facilitative and usually safer, while the former can energize others but also can propel people into situations for which they are not ready. So drawing that line can have heroic or tragic consequences.

Building on a personal experience, "The OD Intervenor" alternates between sketching dark clouds and then suggesting silver linings in this choice between extreme role types. As in the basic orientation of this volume, the selection eventually comes down someplace in between—beyond narrow facilitation, and yet short of all-out aggressive stimulation. In short, variable role playing is often appropriate to the broad range of situations OD intervenors will encounter.

The final selection also directly confronts the OD intervenor with role-tensions that are built into the job, given that many other areas of life pose similar dilemmas and choices. The title of this final selection should be graphic enough to indicate what it attempts to do—"ODers as Servants of Power: Temptations and Countertendencies."

Graphic title or not, a few comments may help orient the reader. ODers often are in highly leveraged situations. If nothing else, ODers are typically seen as keepers of values that most people seem to prefer, even if many of those people also believe it is unrealistic to follow those values in practice. Hence the multiple bonds inherent in the OD specialist preaching greater openness and not overtly restricting situations of "I know something but I can't tell."

The usual situation goes far beyond "if nothing else," of course. For example, ODers typically become privy to information that was either tightly-held or was even unrecognized, and hence is valuable—not only in terms of knowledge useful for helping, but also in terms of power and dollars.

From both perspectives, the specific dimensions of "confidentiality" have a transcending significance in OD.

26

"A Statement of Values and Ethics . . ."

Major recent progress has been made toward the development of a clear professional identity for individuals involved in planned organizational change. The most signal expression of this progress appears in "A Statement of Values and Ethics for Professionals in Organization and Human Systems Development," an effort given basic leadership by Bill Gellerman and Mark Frankel, especially encouraged in its later developmental stages by Don Cole and the Organization Development Institute.

Like all of life, promise in this case must acknowledge and overcome the real potential for mischief. Brief attention will be given to both promise and potential for mischief, by way of providing a framework for what seems to be a helpful developmental process, nicely conceived and off to a good start.

Two promises dominate in the development of "A Statement. . . ." Overall, the goal is to raise the level of what is considered ethical professional practice. Relatedly, this involves two kinds of emphases. The immediate focus is on increasingly clear criteria for thoughtfully encompassing those policies and values considered central to the practice. Discussion of such criteria with many stakeholders has begun, and gaining broad agreement about increasingly targeted versions of the Statement will take years, no doubt. Much later, the focus may shift—even more thoughtfully, or perhaps prayerfully for those with such a bent—to the exclusion in the future of some individuals purporting to practice the professional art-cum-science.

The pitfalls of moving toward professional status also are well-known. This effort might be just another case of protectionism of turf and practice, of keeping out eligible others. Or premature and unwise circumscriptions of the field might choke it even as they sincerely seek to provide protection.

No conclusions are yet obvious concerning the balance of promises and pitfalls that will be generated by the Statement and its developmental process, but several points seem clear enough to this Process Observer even at this early time. Six points deserve special emphasis.

First, the Statement can build on a substantial history that had its limiting features even as it accomplished vital spade work. The pathfinding NTL of the late 1960s and early 1970s was busy struggling to succeed in programmatic senses, and could—and probably should—devote little attention to professional identification or certification issues. The OD Network early on became oriented toward mass membership oriented and constituted a critical homebase for many practitioners. But it did more easy-including than conceptual defining of the field. If anything, indeed, this y'all feel welcome ODN approach contributed to a blurring of the boundaries of OD. But that is not the worst of outcomes, among which can be numbered the ossification of the field. And the International Association of Applied Social Scientests, or IAASS—more lately Certified Consultants International, or CCI—made several brave leaps forward in personal certification, but more recently seems to have lost a critical bulk of its membership and simultaneously induced a sense of the blahs in many who remain on the rolls, hoping for better days. CCI is now defunct, although several of its regional associations propose to continue business as usual.

Second, the Statement seems to have about the correct focus as to its essential professional target members. Note 2 of the Statement purposes:

> The field we call Organization and Human System Development (OD/HSD) is most generally recognized by the name Organization Development (OD) since most of its practitioners focus primarily on organizations. It is also known by the names Change Facilitation, Human Resource Development, Human Systems Development (because the profession works with such diverse systems as individuals, families, communities, and even more inclusive systems) and Applied Behavioral Science (since the profession bases much of its practice on applying the sciences of psychology, sociology, anthropology, and other behavioral sciences).

Third, the work on the Statement is strategically situated. Major actors succeeded in getting a substantial NSF grant, and (in part) the project is housed at a university in a Center for the Study of Ethics in the Professions. Such contextual factors provide some buffering against the kind of forces that impacted adversely on earlier actors in OD's moves toward professional status. Thus NTL faced the practical issues of keeping its members happy with programmatic assignments, while also recognizing those few who were most active in bringing home the bacon of new clients and contracts. Moreover, the OD Network was reasonably responsive to broad membership needs for connecting and for fiesta as well as building skills, but this integrating market niche could not be easily expanded to encompass the differentiation implied by a focus on ethics and values. Finally, IAASS/CCI had to rely on revenue from memberships and on goodwill to support its activities, so that an extensive program of heightening professional consciousness required either a large membership or very high dues. Limits on both existed, so that "extensive program" never developed.

Fourth, the Statement seems reasonably positioned, resting as it does on reasonable aspirations and on a realistic view of its multiple publics. The Statement is the "*beginning* of an educational code," basically, and not a regulatory code. In this regard, the early NTL probably did not reach far enough. Probably, also, IAASS/CCI initially overreached the aspirations of a membership large enough to support it financially. Time will tell whether the Statement's reach will be paired with a useful grasp.

Fifth, the Statement seems nicely articulated with plans for the future that stress the participation by and involvement of various relevant publics, which is clearly appropriate for an OD initiative but has not been characteristic of most past efforts at OD institution building. Immediately, several professional meetings will feature sessions that focus on interpretations of the Statement, in the context of case studies that capture common ethical and value dilemmas. Such sessions were first held at 1985 meetings of the OD Institute and the OD Network, for example, and other sessions have been scheduled. Later still, in the view of this Process Observer, the products of this process might well serve as the working papers for an OD congress or synod for assessing the breadth of consensual support for further efforts to define what it is that we do, when, how, and especially to what standards of excellence.

Sixth, now may be a very good time for the Statement and its associated dynamics. If Terrence Krell is approximately correct in his view of OD as a "maturing product line," for example, separating the baby from the bathwater may be necessary today, even vital. A separate essay deals with the point and some of its intricacies. See the following "Not Whether to Market, But What" for some details. Here note only that the job of protecting the core of OD from such unhappy indiscriminance may be more difficult even a short time from today, if not impossible.

Why this concern about today and the pessimism about tomorrow when it comes to the "OD baby" and the "bathwater" of its present stage of development? "Mature product lines" tend toward competition between suppliers that features, among other elements: a certain untethered ebullience about claims of efficacy; price-cutting rather than quality assurance; a focus on appearance versus substance, as in cosmetic "product differentiation"; and milking product lines rather than putting resources into research and development. These elements imply too much living on past achievements and far too little on "putting something back in the pot."

A sharp contrast seems appropriate, on balance. In earlier days, a strong concern about the details of the who and what and why of planned change may have been viewed as "raining on somebody's parade," as diminishing the enthusiasm and resources that not only had made great progress but also could generate future breakthroughs. Today, future breakthroughs may more nearly be said to require care—even scrupulousness—about what "it" is, who does ''it,'' and why. The Statement encourages such care, and not only at about the correct time but also carried by a process for moving still further that has a good chance to build growing consensus as it goes.

Note

1. For the latest version of the Statement, see Mark S. Frankel, ed., *Values and Ethics in Oganization and Human Systems Development* (Washington, D.C.: American Association for the Advancement of Science, 1987), 69–104.

27

Not Whether to Market, But What

The age of marketing innocence in OD surely extended at least into the early 1970s. Things were being done; competencies were being sharpened and knowledge was being extended; and some money was being made. But the general tone was, if not casual, at least diffused and relaxed. For one thing, most of the OD pioneers had a secure institutional base from which they operated—typically at a university, in which they were tenured or tenurable—and hence in a real sense were innovators whose overhead costs were taken care of. Perhaps paramountly, the emphasis was definitely on research and development rather than on production, let alone marketing. Most early OD savants were at least interested in research, and many were primarily engaged in producing it.

Marketing often did not get due attention, in short. Many saw it as an evasion of the central issues, in fact, if not unworthy of attention.

Times have definitely changed, as Krell so artfully reminds us with his analysis of OD via one marketing concept.[1] OD is a "mature product line," Krell explains, or at least threatens to be. Briefly, this means that demand for OD services may still be growing but not in proportion to the burgeoning of service providers, who increasingly have only one arrow in their occupational quiver. And this kind of "maturity" often has been associated with a host of awkward marketing strategies. The genre is illustrated by: energetic but often overstated product differentiation, an overexuberance about product claims and quick fixes, an off-the-shelf emphasis rather than designing for specifically diagnosed situations, and price-cutting.

Now, one can question Krell's analysis at points. Thus I believe that OD maturity in the marketing sense is a threat only if we lack reasonable wit and will. The traditional turf still permits very great expansionism. Witness the still infrequent extensions into retrenchment and cutback that permit a robust complement to OD's historic emphasis on growth. Even the darkest clouds can have a silver lining.

But there seems little doubt to me that Krell's emphasis on marketing is an apt one, and especially because it provides an orientation and technology to help prescribe for our future as well as to describe it. This space does not permit anything more than a few illustrations, but several points may usefully be kept in mind in any shift of attention—away from whether to market OD, and toward what is being marketed.

First, OD is basically a commitment to a set of humanistic values about desirable patterns of relationships between persons as well as between people and their work. "Traditional OD" was right-on in this particular, Krell advises. Early ODers were likely to view their primary goal as creating more satisfying and productive societies or cultures, with an instrumental interest in designs or learning approaches as mere vehicles for moving toward desired and desirable collective ends. Typically, early ODers tied their mechanics to the vision of a just society, often with democratic overtunes, and always toward the goal of creating greater responsible freedom.[2] In what he calls "mainline OD," Krell sees a definite shift in today's focus—from normative ends to narrow effectiveness or narrower efficiency, from the humanist vision to the portfolio of canned programs. To Krell, mainline OD is "big business" far more than it is a humanistically oriented effort to change our organizational world.

Recognizing this point will be harsh medicine. For crowding all manner of things under the OD tent had several motivations, one of which sought to create (to risk coining a phrase) a common market by association. So those concerned about OD maturity may be distressed by the present prescription for greater selectivity. Differentiation is less fun than aggregation; moreover, it is less likely to generate excitement, even if pain can be generally avoided.

Put more directly, Krell's analysis implies the need for greater in-group/out-group differentiation, as by certification or licensing processes. Opinions have differed zestfully on this point, of course. The emphasis on in/out decisions has ranged from reasonably rigorous in Certified Consultants International, to most casual in the Organization Development Network.

I do not see the differences between "traditional OD" and "mainline OD" as sharply as Krell does, but he may be correct. If so, the value differences need to be clearly staked out and in/out decisions made on what is after all *a* central issue—I would say *the* central issue. Ideally, the differentiation should be mutual, which implies the need for a kind of OD congress or synod, and the sooner the better. But the OD tent simply cannot cover all that has been crowded beneath it. Perhaps most directly, for example, take two applications of job enrichment. One may be OD while the other is mindless mimicry, if not deliberate manipulation. The values underlying the applications determine their standing. Job enrichment designs, and *all* others, can be put in the service of a wide range of ends. The designs per se have no clear or consistent normative standing. Hence Albert Speer's use of designs to heighten efficiency and motivation during World War II is both technologically compatible with today's OD and normatively contemptuous of OD's value traditions.[3] Similarly, one can defile group processes[4] as well as use them as engines for approaching desired and desirable goals.

Second, the core historic technology for approaching OD values is process analysis. This directs attention to the "how" of human interaction, so as to facilitate movement toward a relatively specific set of better relationships. As noted, any technology without values is an unguided missile. We know this central point in our heads, of course, but we can forget it in the rush of life, especially when self-interest is too dominant. Hence the emphases on healthier, more congruent, or more fulfilling systems are necessary normative tethers, as well as metaphors concerning aspirations and ideals.

Third, people often exist in the context of organizational structures and procedures as well as human relationships. The fixation on the latter is not only limiting, but is likely to be a long-run loser to prevailing structures and procedures whose typical antecedents lay in rational-technical myopias such as the "machine model" or the Taylorian one-best way.

Two alternatives can guide OD development in connection with this third point. One is tough, but promises to open new doors as well as to drastically expand the OD market. ODers have to integrate technical skills for designing jobs and organizations with interaction-centered perspectives. The other alternative requires only a facilitative posture, fixating on interaction and relationships. Convenience aside, the business the latter approach elicits seems to me a long-run snare and delusion. In many cases, moreover, the interaction-centered approach may be counterproductive even in the short run and intermediate run. Interaction-centered designs may raise expectations that are dashed against the cold realities of incompatible organization structures and policies.

The easier strategy has a Band-Aid quality, with cooling-out overtones. In this view, OD efforts are basically triggered by breakdowns in rational and technical systems or, in more imaginative versions, are utilized to ease the installation of such systems. Here the OD role is basically facilitative, if not narrowly manipulative.

The tougher strategy involves infusing with OD values and perspectives the several traditional approaches that deal with organizational structures and procedures. This can be done either by diffusion of the values to other specialists, but more desirably by ODers who integrate within their own heads such interests and skills.

Both approaches have worked most successfully in "enrichment" approaches to job analysis and design, but the vision here reaches to the far-fuller panoply of system-influencing disciplines and occupations: accountancy, wage-and-salary administration, employee relations, collective bargaining, and so on.

No sense of any easy piece is appropriate. Only a small part of the required task has been attempted, and this after years of pounding away at establishing that mutual satisfaction of human needs and organizational requirements could come through job design. Even in the case of job design and especially

QWL efforts, moreover, the initiative now has slipped largely into technocratic hands, although the primary initiative came largely from such ODers as Argyris.

So the time is ripe to reassert OD's historical emphases, but this time as much in practice as in theory and philosophy. In sum, a successful initiative of the kind envisioned no doubt will require a major stretch by numerous OD intervenors—into systems analysis, human factors engineering, compensation procedures and systems, and especially into practices and theories of accounting and budgeting. Strong advocacy and architectural roles will be required, in addition, and many ODers emphasize a mostly facilitative role. But most significant in the challenge this essay proposes we undertake, the approach requires integrating OD with some traditional functions or activities. Oppositely, OD is presently feeling full of itself in successfully having generated separate programs: a Master's in Organization Development, or some such.

Difficulties will exist, then, but the bottom line has a compelling quality. If OD is marketed in the three senses sketched above, I see no insurmountable problems. If it is marketed in other ways, we have only ourselves to blame.

Notes

1. Terence C. Krell, "The Marketing of Organization Development: Past, Present, and Future," *Journal of Applied Behavioral Science* 17 (July 1981): 309–23.
2. For example, see Kenneth Benne, "From Polarization to Paradox," 216–47, in Leland Bradford, Jack Gibb, and Kenneth Benne, eds., *T-Group Theory and Laboratory Method* (New York: Wiley, 1964).
3. Ethan A. Singer and Leland M. Wooton, "The Triumph and Failure of Albert Speer's Administrative Genius," *Journal of Applied Behavioral Science* 12 (Jan. 1976): 79–103.
4. For illustrative chapter and verse, see Gene Church and Conrad D. Carnes, *The Pit: A Group Encounter Defiled* (New York: Outerbridge and Lazard, 1972). Among the training aids were a cross, a coffin, oxygen bottles, and piano wire, all in service of the motto: "We'll do anything to help you, even if it means hurting you."

28

Does OD Sufficiently Honor Its Past?

A healthy area of interest and identification may be viewed as in rooted motion. The area's central core should at once recognize its posterity, and also should support a leading edge that continuously seeks to test and (when necessary) to transcend what it honors. Put in other terms, a healthy profession creates at its center a kind of rolling tension between the "line" of aspiration drawn by the pioneers, and the more current simultaneous attempts to extend practice to that "line" as well as to develop a higher level of aspiration.

In these simplified terms, I have a nagging and growing suspicion that things could be far better in today's OD. Worse than not honoring our posterity, *the* problem may lay more in not recognizing that posterity. And that constitutes a far-tougher problem.

Now, what on earth does this ominous even if suitably tentative suspicion imply? Four points may suffice here to sketch a working answer to this query. Note that I will conveniently use affirmative or assertive formulations to express the present position. The reader can mentally add such caveats to each of the five statements below: "Too much evidence suggests that . . . ."; "I am increasingly troubled by . . .."; "One is tempted to conclude, despite only partial and selective evidence, that . . . .", and so on.

First, OD does not recognize its posterity. The neglect appears in various forms: e.g., in reinventing the wheel, and in leaping on bandwagons for this year's variety of sheep-dip before that of past years has been given appropriate trial. And note that my criteria for recognition *do not* require that ODers need to learn—to choose a fanciful example—about people like Bluma Zeigarnik or her "Zeigarnik effect," even though such knowledge seems to me a reasonable indicator of a detailed knowledge of the Gestalt or field psychology so prominent in OD's development.

Let me focus on an exotic form of the issue rather than its garden varieties. This possible sign of the times comes from a professional setting, and involves those who had "made it" as intervenors in the terms in which the world usually makes such judgments—hefty daily fees. The talk turned to intervention strategy, and I remarked: "That's the kind of issue J. J. Rousseau loved to deal with." Memory banks were quickly scanned by my colleagues, and misplaced recognition appeared in one set of eyes. Hands clapped: ''Oh yeah! J. J.! Dy-no-mite!'' My colleagues understood, but it took me awhile to attain wisdom in this apparently small but revealing matter. I referred to Jean Jacques, but my colleague's referent was a TV show about a black family with a beanpole youth named JJ or perhaps Jay-Jay. Such a twain is unlikely to meet, whether in matters great or small.

Second, OD does not honor its posterity. Respecting this point does not require that we posthaste institute an OD Hall of Fame, although that is not a half-bad idea, it seems to me. But we certainly could do a lot better. For example, major commemoration of Kurt Lewin followed some 40 years after his death, and even that was in an NTL context when it could have more heavily involved ODN or CCI.

But, hey, we may be getting better at it. Lee Bradford was fortunately still alive when his contributions were signally recognized, if perhaps fifteen years too late. And the OD Institute and ASTD also have begun to recognize their own before they make their final intervention.

Third, OD does not connect with its posterity. The effect here is illustrated by what occurred at an NTL national meeting perhaps five to seven years ago. One design for connecting called for meetings ''between the generations'' of NTL members. More or less, three or four such ''generations'' were identified, and this covering a period of less than twenty years! The apparent segmentation has diverse roots, but the main effect is consistent—it complicates that linking of ''generations'' required for a strong core that rests on its posterity, to joyfully risk a pun, but only to rise above it, as necessary.

A word or two about this rapid circulation of the generations in OD. Such an effect places an increasing premium on non–face-to-face modes of linking, and contrasts sharply with the early days. Then, the faithful often gathered in proportionately substantial numbers—as at Bethel—and for longish periods. The word got around, as it were. Moreover, most of the old hands also were academics, accustomed to living by the printed word. So the clan knew another—often by sight and direct observation, and almost always by contact through the literature.

Times changed, radically and rapidly. Now many more people are doing so many more things, at higher levels of sophistication.

ODers have not kept pace with the need to evolve more formal ways of linking. Indeed, they often have a bias against such formalization. We are far removed from the charming but sharply limiting exubberance of the 1960s which devalued even faintly formal modes of transmitting knowledge and experience as ''intellectual bullshit.'' So it is not fair to accuse ODers of being ''beyond reason''—a charge that had a modicum of merit when directed at those early interaction specialists, the T-Group trainers. But neither are ODers gung-ho for ''reading the literature.'' Indeed, for a variety of reasons, proportionately more ODers are *less able* to read the literature even if they want to do so, just as it is more necessary to do so. In part, this results from the rapidly changing character of the literature and its burgeoning sources, either of which can overwhelm. Not only is there much more to read, in short, general reading skills and attitudes often will not suffice to cope with technical materials. Moreover, many—probably most—of today's ODers come from nonacademic sources—the ministry, or whatever—and their interpersonal skills often are not complemented (or even lightly burdened) by methodological interests and knowledge of the literature. One might even argue that OD's common emphases on the here and now and the intervenors' ''warm body'' contribute to a mobilization of bias that undercuts attention to the past/future.

So reading has to be today's dominant mode of linking with posterity, but it has become an increasingly chancy medium.

Fourth, ODers do not sufficiently respect their posterity in the most caring way—by testing it and thereby risking the need to transcend it.

How to do better? Many initiatives would help, but one tangible example will have to do to illustrate the genre. Intervenors might routinely devote some greater proportion of their time/dollars to research. This might be done, let us say, by adding 2 to 5 percent to the cost of each contract in an effort to improve the breed. Individual intervenors might do the research or—better still, from several perspectives—they could hire sophisticated third parties to handle this meeting-in-action of the most profound way of honoring posterity. This involves taking their work so seriously as to extend its initiatives, or even to risk subverting them.

29

The Fund for Displaced ODers

During the days of early integration in the South, one Protestant denomination moved in a useful way to moderate a wicked normative dilemma. The denomination's leadership at once believed in racial equality but was often stymied in its sincere intent to move in that direction by an equally strong and longstanding belief in the preeminence of local congregations.

In brief summary, most of the denomination's congregations were quite solid in having little positive regard for integration as an ideal, and these congregations had precious little energy for seeking it in their religious practice. In a few congregations, integration could generate a majority of supporters, but bitter warfare would be common even in those churches if some program of action were instituted locally, and resistance probably would be great even in supportive congregations if the local action were inspired—not to mention directed—by the denomination's leadership. Moreover, since the leadership accepted the norm of local action, covert or "behind the barn" action by them to motivate integration was not deemed appropriate.

How could the religious leadership resolve its dilemma? The full program cannot be reviewed here, but one aspect of their response deserves note. With foundation support, a Fund for Displaced Pastors was set up. Denominational pastors often were replaced by their congregations, for various reasons. The leadership added a useful wrinkle. Any pastor alleging that removal was due to a congregation's dislike of that pastor's prointegration attitudes or behaviors now had an avenue of recourse. An application could be made to a board sympathetic to evidence that a congregation's racial preferences led to a pastor's replacement.

Only one major qualification hedged the continued payment of a pastor's salary, once the board found a prejudicial situation. The pastor had to remain in the congregation's area, continuing to minister as best the pastor could to all within the congregation and its locality.

I have come to learn that similar arrangements exist, even if they are far from commonplace. I am informed that supportive relationships of the same general kind exist among some psychologists under the gun from clients for adhering to professional standards. Moreover, perhaps surprisingly, an association of chemists provides similar support for fellow professionals if certain prejudicial actions at work are taken against them, as by an employing organization that encourages a scientist to fudge results for some reason—as in suppressing a quality-control problem—and then variously disciplines the chemist for the latter's unwillingness to get along by going along.

No doubt this catalog could be extended with more search.

A good idea does not have to be widespread, however, and it occurs to me that now is an appropriate time for considering some such safety net for OD professionals.

Why? A brief review of contemporary stirrings provides context for this conclusion. Most directly, April 1985 saw a milestone in the progress toward a coherent professional identity for specialists in system change. Under the leadership of Bill Gellerman, complex networking has led to "A Statement of Values and Ethics for Professionals in Organization and Human System Development," some details about which appear in the immediately preceding essay. Moreover, another important stage of evolution in OD's professional identity began in May 1985, with Mark Frankel providing special guidance. The Statement will be discussed at various professional meetings, with the focus being on the analysis and discussion of case studies as a way of beginning the processes of acquainting colleagues with how the Statement's provisions might apply in specific action-settings. The first of many go-arounds was held at the fifteenth annual Information Sharing meeting sponsored by the Organization Development Institute at Lake Geneva, whose continuing interest has been fueled and fanned by Don Cole over some inhospitable years. The cases and their accompanying reactions will subsequently be published, both in articles and in a book, by way of making available to interested others the essence of this round of public presentations.[1]

The connection of these useful stirrings and The Fund for Displaced ODers should not be obscure. In effect, and certainly none too soon in the view of this Process Observer, the Statement seeks to heighten the level of consciousness about ethical and value issues, about what it is that we do, why, and how. Overall, practice should profit from the greater coherence provided by the educative strategy underlying the Statement, and by discussions about how the Statement's provisions apply in specific settings.

In a few cases, however, the Statement also may induce a conflict between a practitioner and an employing organization. This likely effect needs to be addressed early, directly, and forcefully. For the Statement encourages high standards of ethical performance, and it would be cavalier to neglect the crosspressures that no doubt will be induced in some cases as successes in that basic intent to raise standards are achieved. It is in the nature of such matters that some early advocates will pay a price to vivify the Statement.

The least that we can do is to ease some of the pain by providing for a safety net. Enter, stage center, The Fund for Displaced ODers as one approach to mitigating possible conflicts for professionals.

The Statement should heighten consciousness about ethical problems, in short, and this may surface new problems, or exacerbate old problems, for OD practitioners, and especially for internal consultants. The Fund would provide one approach to respecting the Statement while acknowledging some concrete sharing in the burdens that individuals may come to experience because they respect the Statement. Ethical issues would not only be faced more squarely but, in the longer run, this greater forthrightness might have the effect of moderating the real temptations to risk ethical shortcuts, or to accept an authority figure's encouragement or order to an ODer to engage in questionable activities.

The temptation is to plunge into details about this germ of an idea, and perhaps even to make a splashy pledge to get the financial ball rolling.

Quick second thoughts tether such overenthusiasms, however. Bad enough, they would be grandstanding. Moreover, the professional infrastructure needs to develop in collective and consensual modes.

So temptation will be resisted, at this time. Hopefully, fellow professionals will accept The Fund as one idea that will get its share of attention in the useful ferment that should follow in the wake of the publication of the April 1985 version of "A Statement of Values and Ethics for Professionals in Organizations and Human Systems Development." We shall see, and hope, and try to nudge developments here and there along the way.

Note

1. For a brief history of the project and its products, see Mark S. Frankel, ed., *Values and Ethics in Organization and Human Systems Development* (Washington, D.C.: American Association for the Advancement of Science, 1987).

30

What *In Search of Excellence* Still Needs to Seek, and How OD Can Help

Without a doubt, *In Search of Excellence*[1] is a bona fide blockbuster among books on management, or almost any other category, for that matter. Consider only one indicator of impact. The Peters and Waterman volume has sold, by far, more copies than all of Peter Drucker's numerous books taken together. Where it will end, moreover, no one can be certain. A *Business Week* article led to *the* book, the book begat a flock of lectures—first in person, and then video-aided—and now a serialized set of management development materials has been prepared to still more conveniently extend the message.

Like many human works of higher orders of magnitude, it is not apparent what all the fuss is about. Successful American firms in selected categories are said to be characterized by "strong" cultures, to provide a straight vanilla summary, with several more or less similar characteristics. The descriptions are colorful and spritely, and the volume abounds with anecdotes about heroes and heroic myths. And the book is "good news from America,"[2] which may in the final analysis explain the volume's unprecedented reception in terms of a basic hunger to be better and to have local models for doing so.

Why these descriptions should have attracted major attention is anyone's guess, however. The authors express basic surprise that so many would care, so intensely, for example.[3] And if that is not enough support of the present point, more convincing evidence is easy to assemble. Thus it far more clear how the authors came to their conclusions, from whom they obtained their data, how "excellent" companies are defined, or even which firms are studied.[4]

These formidable questionables may be illustrated. The basic lessons that form the heart of the volume, one critic notes, "were presumably drawn from either the 36- or 62-company sample."[5] This suggests a certain methodological flexibility, of course. Moreover, it appears that a large proportion of

157

the firms in the research panel—at least 21/62nds, or perhaps even 21/36ths—were included in the panel without meeting the volume's explicit criteria for choice. Seven of the additions were "estimated" to have met the financial criteria[6]; and the fourteen other additions may have been made *after* the characteristics of well-managed firms were identified, although the wording admits several interpretations. Specifically, the fourteen additions are "a group of exemplars which, without benefit of specific selection criteria, do seem to represent especially well both sound performance and the eight traits we have identified."[7]

These crucial methodological curiosities aside, the success of *In Search of Excellence* at once surpasses easy understanding and—since the *right* word does not come easily, an approximation will have to do—may be dangerous.

As for surprise, the basic position that "strong" cultures and similarities between them are proposed to characterize excellent firms, however defined, does not constitute news. The general point of the significance of "culture" could hardly escape the least-assiduous student in a whole gamut of introductory versions of academic courses—social psychology, delinquency, social organization, and management, among others. That has been standard fare for a very long time. In the specialized literature, the critical role of culture in effective organizations was comprehensively demonstrated by many, again a long time ago. Thus Selznick[8] masterfully wrote of the centrality of infusing with value the various technical systems in organizations. The business executive Barnard also developed a similar position in a well-known book[9]; and many, many others have developed aspects of the significance or organizational cultures. The essential point is pretty much the same in all these formulations. Individuals tend to have strong needs for belonging and for interpreting what they do and how they think in terms of broader meanings, and culture provides precisely just this transcendence of self, of everyday and often banal activities.

Now consider the danger of *In Search of Excellence's* treatment of culture. The conventional view stresses that cultures of efficient organizations can be good, bad, or indifferent when viewed from a broader value perspective. In the usual formulation, cultures can be efficient and/or effective, with the criteria in the first case being narrow input/output ratios and in the latter case emphasizing broad social and moral evaluations. Thus the culture of the Mafia or Cosa Nostra was "strong" and, at least for a substantial period, that system was efficient but not effective by conventional social and legal mores.

Hence generations of commentators have insisted that cultures must be differentiated. In OD, for example, the historic focus has been on developing a *specific appropriate* culture, rather than on any "strong" culture. As the late Alexander Winn explains about the intended culture underlying OD:[10]

> The term "organization development" . . . implies a normative, re-education
> strategy intended to affect systems of beliefs, values and attitudes within the
> organization so that it can adapt better to the accelerated rate of change in tech-
> nology, in our industrial environment and society in general.

In Search of Excellence walks a very narrow line with respect to the need to differentiate cultures, beyond such gross descriptors as "strong." Specifically, *In Search of Excellence* neither proposes that a culture is a culture, nor does it specify the detailed properties of normatively appropriate cultures. To be sure, *In Search* does propose that well-run firms have numerous people programs, for example. But they could be motivated by an essential desire to manipulate unilaterally as well as by an intent to contribute to human growth and development. Which it is, or in what combinations, does make a difference.

Rather than specify appropriate cultural values, Peters and Waterman issue a warning about cultures, albeit a very brief one. Given their strong need for meaning and belonging, humans may surrender too much of themselves, too quickly, the authors note, and this might even lead to expressions-in-action of the "darker side of our nature."[11] As Peters and Waterman conclude: ". . . the more worrisome part of a strong culture is the very present possibility of abuse."[12] They cite the "frightening" results of two experiments—the widely known work of Milgram[13] and Zimbardo's equally ominous "Stanford Prison" experiment[14]—as illustrations of the fearsome potential of our "darker side." The basic bulwark against this worst-case outcome, Peters and Waterman conclude, are the "customers," who presumably will stop buying a firm's products if they suspect that the "frightening" features of that firm's culture have become prominent.

Hence the potential danger of *In Search of Excellence*. Careless readers may retain the glorification of "strong" cultures even as those readers neglect the efficiency/effectiveness distinction, despite the warning of Peters and Waterman. And "customers" may unevenly perform the critical role that Peters and Waterman assign them—that of cultural police.

So how can OD help? Clearly, OD has been in the business of contributing to the development of what *In Search* needs—in general, OD focuses of increasing responsible freedom at work; and more specifically, OD helps create cultures at work that are loaded with quite specific values. So one linkage between OD and that book is quite prominent.

On the face of it, however, this is help that *In Search* probably would prefer to do without. The book not only neglects OD, but demeans aspects of it.[15] This is most curious in one sense—many of *In Search*'s cadre of well-managed firms now support, or did support, extensive OD efforts. And those efforts often concentrate on inducing the very feature that *In Search* sees as fundamental in well-managed firms with tight cultures—a substantial degree of interpersonal and intergroup trust. To be a bit catty, perhaps, *In Search* provides few clues as to how that much-desired level of trust is achieved in some firms, but not others.

Notes

1. Thomas J. Peters and Robert H. Waterman, Jr., *In Search of Excellence: Lessons From America's Best-Run Companies* (New York: Harper & Row, 1982).
2. *Ibid.*, xxv.
3. *Ibid.*, 25.
4. For a critical analysis of these and other features, see Robert T. Golembiewski, "Toward Excellence in Public Management," 177–198, in Robert B. Denhardt and Edwin T. Jennings, Jr., eds., *Toward a New Public Service* (Columbia, MO: University of Missouri Press, 1987).
5. Daniel T. Carroll, "A Disappointing Search for Excellence," *Harvard Business Review* 61 (Nov. 1983): 78.
6. See Peters and Waterman, *In Search of Excellence*, 23n.
7. *Ibid.*, 24.
8. Philip Selznick, *Leadership in Administration* (New York: Harper & Row, 1957).
9. Chester I. Barnard, *The Functions of the Executive* (Cambridge, Mass.: Harvard University Press, 1967).
10. Alexander Winn, " The Laboratory Approach to Organization Development." Paper presented at the Annual Converence, British Psychological Society, Oxford, England, Sept. 1968).
11. Peters and Waterman, *In Search of Excellence*, 78.
12. *Ibid.*, 78.
13. Stanley Milgram, *Obedience to Authority* (New York: Harper & Row, 1974).
14. Consult the introduction to Christina Maslach, *Burnout: The Cost of Caring* (Englewood Cliffs, N.J.: Prentice-Hall, 1982).
15. *In Search of Excellence*, 241–42.

31

Some Unintended
Consequences of Intervening
"Where the Pain Is"

One of the more frequent and well-advised truisms encourages that OD intervenors seek out pain, trauma, and discrepancies between actual conditions and ideas, all the better to function in that "facilitator" role so prominent in OD how-to-do books. The reasons are clear. The pain or discrepancy not only can provide the motivational energy necessary for unfreezing, but that energy can also encourage choice and possible change. And the facilitator role has much to recommend it, especially in the senses of maximizing the probabilities of client ownership of any learning, as well as minimizing the chances of charismatic but misguided ODers precipitating a naive client into awkward situations. So the common advice is reasonable, as far as it goes.

Like all simple and sovereign prescriptions, however, this one has real problems when it is taken straight, undiluted by at least native cunning and uninformed by solid theoretical orientations. This essay draws attention to some of the unintended consequences of this good thing extended too far, and it also suggests some primary defenses against "good enough" coming to be "too bad." Paradoxically, the problems grow in direct proportion with our increasing knowledge about, and substantial success rates with, a range of OD interventions. In short, OD intervenors know more and more about how to have an impact, and that implies an increasing potential for good *or* ill. So the focal issues will probably get more rather than less intense as time passes.

Let us simplify by developing a scenario, beginning with the ringing of an ODer's phone. The scenario begins like this:

> Hello, Bob, this is Ed White with Global. We're about ready to start a new campaign, and I'm anxious that my folks are with me. I believe things are OK, but I can't risk any glitches. And every once in a while I hear grumbles about my team from my team.
>
> I understand you do team-building. Can you help?

A contract is subsequently struck, and the intervenor diagnoses a simple case of disagreement and not the more subtle "crisis of agreement," and a straightforward confrontation design followed by contracting is utilized. As is typically the case, in a day and a half or so, both manager and subordinates get better perspective on each other, and several psychological contracts are entered into. All goes well enough for awhile but, all too soon, the consultant learns on an informal follow-up visit that some slippage has occurred, and especially on the manager's part. Subordinates conclude things may be a bit better than they were before, but not very much. Moreover, they feel used, and report they will be less eager to "play the contracting game" the next time around. Consultant gets to the manager, who volubly and good-naturedly thanks the consultant and notes, abstractly:

> You know I really appreciate your following-up, and on your own, too. That's caring, with hustle added. But our budget is tight right now, and there will be better times to look at our team relationships. I'll give you a call—count on it. Thanks again.

The ODer departs a bit sadly, having heard that one before. That phone call may well come, but the odds are strong that it will come when relationships have deteriorated to touchy if not destructive levels.

This common scenario leaves the OD intervenor wondering about which of several interpretations apply, and none of them are attractive. To sample the major possibilities:

- ODers might be encouraged not to be "too good." For example, there might be a temptation to create a kind of "optimal dependency" by the client—not enough to undercut psychological ownership of the results, but enough to encourage client responsiveness when revisits seem appropriate.
- The ODer is not permitted back because client concludes a poor job was done, but for various reasons chooses to keep that evaluation from the OD intervenor. Client told the varnished truth simply to be done with consultant in a civil way, but nonetheless affirmatively.
- Managers have short attention spans. A problem reduced to tolerable proportions becomes a problem out of mind. The manager glides on to more pressing matters, riding the recently gained leverage into the ground. The manager will be back to the OD intervenor, but risks being "late."
- The ODer is thought of as a kind of vestal virgin—to be saved for special purposes at delimited times. The ODer will be sought when things again "go critical," which puts the OD intervenor in a Sisyphean role—helping push a rock up a hill, only to have it come crashing down, when a repeat performance is then requested. ODers hence often will start from failure following success, rather than building on success.
- The OD intervenor is used as a cooling-out agent, with the client being somewhere from unaware to fully conscious of an intended manipulation.

Most ODers probably find it easier to understand the former, and even to forgive it. I prefer the latter case of the two, because explicit strategies seem to me to be easier to change, or at least to direct arguments against without generating a host of pious and even hurt disclaimers.

What can the OD intervenor do actively and proactively, to reduce the time and energy spent in such generally unproductive speculations? I suggest four contributors to a working solution. In no particular order, they are as follows.

First, work to set appropriate expectations, and discourage hopeful thought by the client about one-shot designs doing the job forever. As Herb Shepard noted, the OD consultant's first task is to get a client. But it often will be easier on both parties to discourage a client with awkward expectations, upfront and early. So I encourage this modification of Shepard's rule: Some client may be preferable to no client; but ranking far above both is a client with reasonable expectations.

Remember that the intervenor's most powerful intervention is: "No, I do not believe that is a reasonable expectation. If you need to think about one-shot efforts, perhaps another consultant will be better for you."

I know you will lose a few clients this way, but I believe you are certain to gain credibility with most potential clients.

Second, create a field of forces—which I would label "political"—to discourage a client from taking easy ways out later in the game. Convenient ways to do this involve specifically scheduled follow-on activities. I long ago adopted the practice of routinely scheduling a "reinforcement session" about two to four months after a team-building effort to review progress, to share data about the fidelity of meeting contracts, and so on. And Boss argues persuasively for periodic and private sessions with authority figures. The point is the same: work for early commitment to a multistage design, communicate that agreement widely, and let the schedule motivate downstream follow-on while reducing the probability of "easy escapes" by the client.

Third, gather data at regular intervals, especially via standard instruments like Frank Friedlander's Group Behavior Inventory. Such comparative data can facilitate timely intervention, and save intervenors from playing Sisyphean roles.

Fourth, focus on periodic "socioemotional audits" at least as much as episodic team building. This often will involve selling a potential client an unwanted service, but the rationale for such audits is obvious and organization folk have had experience with other kinds of audits. This kind of approach—whether called "audit" or whatever—can get ODers out of a reactive mode, and can reduce the probability of being called in when things are at "rock bottom," to again allude to the frustration and wasted emotion of playing the Sisyphus role.

Notes

1. Robert T. Golembiewski, *Approaches to Planned Change*. (New York: Marcel Dekker, 1979), vol. 1, esp.
2. R. Wayne Boss, "Team Building and the Problem of Regression: The Personal Management Interview as an Intervention." *Journal of Applied Behavioral Science*, 19 (Jan. 1983): 67–83.

32

"Promise Not To Tell":*
A Critical View of "Confidentiality" in
Consultation

It is passing strange, the way apparently disconnected themes lock into one another. Perhaps the reader can share some sense of my pleasant surprise in a recent experience.

Some stage setting is necessary. I was trying to make myself plain to two reviewers about my ideal of "limited confidentiality," in a paper associated with *The Statement of Ethics for Professionals in Organization and Human System Development*. The theme was only part of a piece which the reviewers otherwise viewed charitably, but "limited confidentiality" got to them. One warned ominously of Svengalian power seekers in consultant's guise, as well as of "unwise and improper delegations" by the client. And the other reviewer pointedly concluded that there would be no consulting relationship in our futures, given my sense of restricted confidentiality.

Well, I did what I could in that limited space, but the basic issue still troubled although I went undeflected. How to better and more fully develop my view of the ideal consulting relationship? And how to capture complex distinctions in such a way that the details do not get lost in offensive or defensive rushes of adrenaline? Patently, I needed more space to develop the distinction, but I also needed some vehicle to at least keep the gateways of minds open while that greater space did its thing. Those twin requirements were of special moment because I took the reactions of the two reviewers to be modal, and so in speaking to their concerns, I might better communicate with most of those serious about consultation.

An article was required to do the job and, serendipitously, no sooner had I responded affirmatively to an invitation from Editor Glassman to contribute a piece than I had my title and theme. While skimming several issues of *Consultation*, seeking guidance for a suitable approach, an advertisement for a book caught my eye and my mind—*Promise Not to Tell*, by Carolyn Polese.[1]

That title relates to extreme and tragic behavior—the sexual exploitation of

*Reprinted from *Consultation*, 5 (Spring 1986), 68–76.

children—but it could keep the mental doorway open, for my purposes. Just let that title sift through your mind. How clever of the exploiter to propose: "Promise not to tell." And how basically correct of the author to use that injunction ironically, even sardonically. The title leads the reader to a conclusion as no evidence might: how obviously wicked is unrestricted confidentiality in the case of such a sad relationship.

To be sure, whatever else may be said, consultation is not child exploitation. But this essay will argue that unrestricted confidentiality has awkward implications for both classes of relationships—between consultant and client, as well as between children and adults. Confidentiality can be a very good thing, but it is easy enough to have too much of even the very best things.

Hence the focus here on some of the details of why a consulting relationship is awkwardly guided by the unrestricted pledge: "Promise not to tell." Specifically, three themes will dominate. They involve: general distinctions between two models of confidentiality; some action scenarios involving confidentiality; and an application of the two ideals about confidentiality to the scenarios.

Two Ideal Models of Confidentiality

Two ideal models of confidentiality preoccupy this section. Conveniently, they are designated as unrestricted and limited, although caveats apply in both cases. Even "unrestricted confidentiality" is limited by most observers; and "limited confidentiality" includes unrestricted zones!

1. Unrestricted confidentiality. The dominant view of confidentiality shares a basic kinship with the folk wisdom about the Catholic's historic view of the confessional—intimate materials shared between persons on a prescribed and even sacred turf, with one party ordained for the task of facilitating expiation for sin, with God as the only witness. Every *early* confessional I ever saw also was dark, and the participants talked in hushed tones, even whispered, thus heightening the sense of sharply limited sharing and sacredness.

The "confessional" wears different (even gaudy) raiment nowadays, in most places, but let us not devalue the symbol by the weight of history. The "unrestricted view" of confidentiality in consultation has much in common with the metaphor of the confessional.

Now, most observers acknowledge that confidentiality should not be, and cannot be, absolutely unrestricted, even though many have deep trouble drawing the line. Consider consultant's knowledge of an "imminent evil act," such as a serious quality-control problem that endangers the public health and safety, *right now*, but which management is hiding to buy time and collect dollars while the stock of the product is being depleted. Probably, most consultants would inform appropriate authorities, at least after urging client to do so. The principle of required disclosure is accepted by some professions, e.g., law. However, major interpretive problems exist about what constitutes an "imminent evil act." Consider the psychiatrist who learns from a client of a fantasized or planned murder. The rub here is the degree to which specialists can reasonably predict "action" from verbal disclosures.

At another level, other observers question our general ability *not* to disclose, even when we work hard at it. Few are good enough maskers, or actors, not to signal when someone is getting close to an absolute confidence. And you often learn more from what people do not say, or what they shy away from, than from subjects on which they are voluble.

Such caveats notwithstanding, no doubt that dominant opinion supports a basically unrestricted sense of confidentiality. The world in this view may intrude on the confessional a bit, that is, but not much.

2. Restricted confidentiality.   I am more comfortable with somewhat restricted confidentiality although, admittedly, I cannot with great precision specify beforehand the exact areas where absolute confidentiality will be breached. My locus of action is the complex, systemic consultation in management settings, which place a premium on quick reactions and where absolute confidentiality can be seriously counterproductive.

Let me begin with a caveat. "Restricted confidentiality" includes some of the absolute, or near absolute. "Mum is the word," in short, in some areas. For example, national security issues often qualify, although that concept can be chameleon or charade or both, more useful for keeping information from our friendly fellow countrymen than for keeping it from malevolent others. "Insider information" about a new product or acquisition also cannot be shared, legally as well as ethically, although the word often gets accurately guessed or directly gets around. Personally, also, my respect of unrestricted confidentiality can be engaged when those I work with have strong needs in this regard, either in general or on a specific topic.

While acknowledging these absolute or near-absolute features of confidentiality, I nonetheless have a definite leaning toward restricted confidentiality. Allow me the license of quoting myself, in an effort to give some content to "restricted." My ideal takes this general form, and it applies to both client and consultant although I use the latter perspective here:[2]

> We can go absolutely confidential under explicitly signaled conditions but, in general, I believe we'll both profit if you basically trust in my discretion concerning the *possible and infrequent* use of any information. Generally, I'll try to check with you beforehand when I have the least doubt about using materials, or about whether and how the sources should be disguised.

But sometimes that will not be possible when I believe use of materials is not only prudent but urgent, and when the moment is not likely to be recaptured.

If that makes you nervous, we can talk about why our trust level is not high enough. Maybe a consultative relationship is just not in the cards for us.

The usual notion is that confidentiality develops trust and, of course, it can. The précis above agrees, but adds the crucial caveat that helping make desired things happen also can build trust. Here discretion is a powerful supplement to general confidentiality, given some risk to both client and consultant.

Action Perspectives on Restricted Confidentiality

Since the specific arena for restricted confidentiality cannot be specified beforehand, does that imply a kind of blank check permitting consultant license whenever the whim comes along? I believe not. Two action scenarios may help circumscribe the arena for restriction, to deliberately mix my verbal symbols. Both scenarios not only illustrate hitches with which consultants in large systems must deal, but they also constitute motivators of restricted confidentiality. A following section details some of those motivations.

1. *A deliberately binding disclosure?* Generally, confidentiality is seen as facilitating helpful sharing, which permits consultant a fuller view of the multiple realities typically at issue. And so it can, and so it does. But confidentiality can be deliberately limiting, even hobbling, and perhaps especially in large systems where power dynamics exist, and often dominate.

My case is a simple one, and may—possibly but not likely, in my view—reflect a disclosure that was intended to help. I need not come to a decision about that. But I do know that the disclosure was binding in effect rather than helping, in the context of an agreement—which I unwisely accepted and perhaps even less wisely respected—about strict confidentiality.[3] A co-consultant on a volatile project embraced me after a common triumph, narrowly snatched from debacle or even disaster. "You just earned something I never thought I'd tell you," he said, in referring to our common client X, who hired us independently but liked to work us in tandem. "X's wife is lesbian and an alcoholic, and she has been committed several times," I was told before I could stop my confider. "That will help you understand some of the strange things X does. But if you ever tell X, I'll deny I said it."

Why the immobilization? Let me sketch the pushes and pulls acting on me. Clearly, my preference would be to go to X, to test the point, or at least to share my concern. In my view, given my unwise agreement, I would at least have to inform my co-consultant of my action, and ideally have him present.

Co-consultant's position remains firm, however. He will deny the conversation, whatever my concerns or however expressed.

So I am stymied on the point, as these considerations imply:

- There seems precious little sense to me in going to X and, in effect, saying "Somebody, but I can't tell you who, is saying things about your wife."
- Suppose I identify the inside dopester, who then denies the conversation, as he promises he will do if I ever mention it? That may put me, as the politicals put it so directly, in a pissing contest with a skunk.
- Suppose I identify the source, who denies the conversation and, further, charges or implies that I would be so reckless only because of our differences (real enough) on other issues?
- Is X's affirmation or denial relevant for the organization and its agents, assuming no performance problems and assuming no whispering about X's wife? I doubt it.
- My relationship with X has been kept free—deliberately on his part, I believe—of references to his nonwork situation. Is it my obligation to expand the zone of our relationship? I see no present reason to do so, although I can envision circumstances that would impress that responsibility on me.

But some movement was possible. I successfully distanced myself from the co-consultant—an unsatisfactory but reasonably satisfying effort.

2. The deliciously binding disclosure. I may appear histrionic here, but "deliciously binding" seems right-on to me as a description of a second scenario. That evaluation applies, in part, because I do not believe that the disclosure was "maliciously binding" (although it could have been). Moreover, I knew all along that I could have revealed the disclosure at several points without violating the letter or the spirit of the operative sense of confidentiality.

The scenario begins on a pleasant day overlooking the Pacific. Client Joe had reached a flash point. "If this [action] goes through, I won't last six months. I'm against it, and here are the reasons why."

A day later, discussion in Joe's executive group centers on "the action." Joe is silent as antagonist, but works hard to facilitate the reactions of his subordinates. The antiaction lead is taken by Sam, early and definitely. "No surprise," I make a note to myself. "Joe no doubt told Sam what he told me." I did not have to make a note that the Joe/Sam duo had been both dynamic and decisive over the years. I knew that. Here was another example of their collaboration, I suspected strongly, often spontaneous but perhaps planned in this case.

Slowly, the other subordinates came to a shared conclusion. "We'll take [the action], but we need a substantial financial motivation to take on the pain. No capital gain, no pain!" This was a new factor in "the action," a big-ticket item that Joe had not considered seriously before the meeting.

I got more active here. How preemptive would influential others see this demand? What risks were involved? Was the group as self-satisfied as they seemed to me, having come to a tough decision? Was everyone on board?

Sam was not, determinedly, and Joe said he "could live with it." The latter jolted me, of course.

My mind whirred. Was Sam doing the tough work, and Joe holding back to save himself for other issues? There was a very real probability that the group's demand would be rejected, I realized, even aggressively if not vindictively. Joe might opt not to deflate their enthusiasm at the moment as a learning device. But what was Sam doing?

So I grew concerned about Joe's failure to share with subordinates what he so animatedly revealed to me earlier, but I controlled my concern. Why? Well, the management members might change their minds and their largely unanimous decision. They certainly had done so before, and Joe might even be waiting to see if Sam's continued opposition would erode the agreement. Or Joe might be convinced that the management group's demand would be rejected by prestigious others, and that his executives should be given the opportunity to exercise good judgment under stress.

I remained active, but not disclosing. I continued to "troll with a long line," several times soliciting any reactions or feelings that "might not have been aired in the movement toward a decision." And I tried to make a soul-depth eye contact with Joe each time, but he did not volunteer and I did not publicly remind him or his disclosure to me and (I was confident, in a very great degree) to Sam. I did not feel bound by "absolute confidentiality," but I basically believed that Joe should "make it happen" while Bob G would "let it happen."

"It" never happened during our offsite sessions. In slam-bang order, the management group's demand was accepted in principle by prestigious others. Sam continued to object about taking on "the activity," but Joe did not reveal his going-in conclusion although "given" several "chances" by Bob G.

While we were debriefing, Sam indicated that he was not his usual enthusiastic self, especially about my services, but also about group openness. I thought I knew what he meant—that I had not inspired sufficient openness in Joe. Sam's reaction resulted in a quite jubilant chorus of approval for what they had done, however, and for the role of Bob G. in that achievement. Most were estimating their capital gains, I suppose, a matter of sufficient satisfaction that several participants vowed "to cut me in on the deal." Joe was mostly facilitative.

Shortly thereafter, I learned from others whose word I respect that Sam felt blindsided by both Joe and myself. He was set up to protect Joe's pseudointerest, Sam felt, in front of peers as well as prestigious others. And he was just left there alone, like the proverbial black sheep at a stiff-necked family's reunion.

Almost immediately, I had a session with Joe, with the initial hope of Sam's presence. However, Sam would be far away, at an important offsite. With Joe, I emphasized Sam's alleged reaction and its credibility, from Sam's perspective. Joe confirmed that he had told Sam about his going-in doubts in much the same terms I heard. "You need to get to him quick, and explain why you acted as you did," I advised. The danger, of course, was that Sam's interpretation might propel him into defensive strategies, in spite of the long association of the "dynamic duo."

Joe explained, to my satisfaction, why he was not forthcoming about his despairing conclusion. Initially, he did so to avoid inhibiting discussion, later because he thought there was little chance the group demand would be accepted, and finally so as not to jeopardize the substantial (and unanticipated) financial rewards that might accrue to his subordinates (and himself). I had no doubt that Joe was correct in his estimate that his revelation would have stopped "the activity" cold, at any stage of discussion except perhaps after the assent of prestigious others.

I planned on an early session with Sam, to go over the reasons for my silence about Joe's disclosure, albeit silence paired with aggressive attempts to encourage Joe to tell all concerned about his going-on estimate that he "won't last six months" following the course of action the group had now exuberantly embarked on.

Events intervened, and that session with Sam had to be delayed. But the materials will be shared, whether or not Joe has his session with Sam. Joe understands that, and I hope Sam has come to understand, and even accept, why I did what I did.

Applying Ideals to Scenarios

So what about applying the two ideals to the scenarios? Consider each, in turn.

The case seems open and shut to me for the first scenario. Unrestricted confidentiality was no help; it was more the core of the problem. I agreed to the ground rule, and paid the price. I suspect my chain was being jerked, and also that my discloser "confided" the same information to multiple others. Distancing myself from the discloser was not ideal, but unavoidable for me due to his intransigence.

Unrestricted confidentiality would have required easier choice making in the second scenario, but I see it as of limited utility even so. Even though I did not divulge the disclosure, I always felt I could have, and I almost came to that point a time or two. Of what value was the restricted confidentiality that Joe, Sam, and I agreed existed in this case? "Restricted" here means that we each relied on the discretion of the other about what to reveal and when, given that discretion never would be casual and that we would expect some but not continuing differences of opinion from case to case about what constituted "good" discretion. The question is most salient because, on the surface of it, I *behaved essentially as if confidentiality were absolute.*

Without pretending to completeness, let me sketch several senses in which I see value in bounded confidentiality in the second scenario. In no particular order of importance, consider these advantages:

- Determining the area and degree of restricted confidentiality implies working toward a sharper and more precise understanding by client and consultant—a quality of careful and prudent awareness of the other, beginning with contracting and extending throughout the association.
- Restricted confidentiality implies a goal of evermore precise sharing of goals, strategies, and views of the world between client and consultant, so that consultant interventions reflect increasingly informed choices.
- Each of the choice points for "making it happen"—although I chose not to do so—keep the consultant alive, vital, and checking facts and interpretations. "Checking the map" can lead to modifying or even "redrawing the map."
- Facing choice about disclosure helps induce for consultant a degree of precisely those things client is being helped with—the sense of control over what is happening, a share in the ownership of the process and its consequences, and a vitality associated with meaningful choice. No equality is implied or intended, but what's good for the goose also serves the gander.
- Facing choice about disclosure helps consultant avoid frustration with aspects of the role, as could become manifest in an unconscious effort to influence or control borne of overscrupulosity in trying not to influence or control.
- The choice making can deepen trust. Joe knew I could have pulled the trigger in the presence of both subordinates and higher-ups, but he also knows I did not because of empathy for his role and caution about possible hidden agendas (of which there seem none). Sam came to a similar conclusion, if by a less direct route.
- The choice making by consultant can serve as an important indicator of appropriate openness as well as a stimulant to it. Since Joe knew I knew, he would be biased toward sharing the data publicly, unless serious reasons encouraged not disclosing. Knowing that, after encouraging disclosure, I would have to have *grave* reasons to choose disclosure after observing Joe's lack of response to my overtures. I had concerns, but not grave reasons.

Notes

1. Carolyn Polese, *Promise Not to Tell* (New York: Human Sciences Press, 1985).
2. "The Internal Consultant and Confidentiality," a manuscript to be published by Mark Frankel in association with *Statement of Values and Ethics for Professionals in Organization and Human System Development*, 4–5.
3. Robert T. Golembiewski, *Humanizing Public Organizations* (Mt. Airy, Md.: Lomond Publications, 1985), 309–18.

33

The OD Intervenor:
Wonder Woman/Superman or On-Call
Facilitator?

One session at an annual meeting of the Academy of Management in Atlanta had a profound impact on attendees and panel alike. The topic, as I recall, was: OD Intervenor: Superman or Nebish? I was to make the argument for Intervenor/Superman; and Jerry Harvey was to do the honors for Intervenor/Nebish.

We never really got to the point of any meaningful contrasts/comparisons, in what was to be a session that was to dwell on the advantages and disadvantages of both Superman and Nebish.

What happened? Well, I guess I was in one of my less-restricted moods, for I decided I would *really* do Superman. I got myself one of those S-shirts, you know; and my artful wife even made me a cute little cape that I could tie around my neck to create a curious paradox to the amply-filled S-shirt. I dressed for the occasion—with dark shirt and white tie over the S-shirt, a blue blazer and horn-rim eyeglasses, and with my cape in a briefcase—but I did not know until just after I started that I would do it. The audience was hep. Just seconds into my talk, I deliberately removed and folded my glasses, as Clark Kent would do before his metamorphosis into Superman, and the audience knew—*really knew*—that something other than another convention talk had begun. I removed my tie, then the blazer and dark shirt; and the audience just jiggled with gleeful anticipation. Then I opened my briefcase—talking all the while about the significance of OD intervenor as Superman—and shook out the wrinkles in my red cape and made a delicate bow of its tie-strings.

At about that time, the metaphor really took over. We heard little about OD intervenor as nebish. As I recall, Jerry Harvey discarded his prepared notes on the Intervenor as Nebish and delightedly began exploring the Superman metaphor on-the-fly. The presentations and discussion swirled about the OD intervenor as Superman—sometimes as an attractive metaphor, but often as a symbol that elicited heated and even angry reactions. Sparks flew, and some presenters were not aware of some of the harsh words and judgments that were passed. The session was recorded so—given that the laughter and other reactions at times overwhelmed the presentations and rejoinders—memory did not have to be relied upon.

I have pondered on several occasions the energizing power of the Superman metaphor, for I do not believe my message had such power independent of the S-shirt and the cute little red cape. In abstract, my message was that an OD intervenor can be—indeed, should be—Superman in several specific but limited senses which include these five used here for illustrative purposes:

- "No" is often the most powerful intervention that can be made, and we know with growing precision when "No" is appropriate. Several varieties of "No" can be distinguished:

    "No, I don't believe that intervention is appropriate."

    "No, the available literature suggests that won't work."

    "No, I will not provide OD services because I have real doubts as to the long-run outcomes in your organization, given my reading of your intent and the organization's track record."

    "No, I cannot serve as a resource because it appears to me you want a cooling-out experience only."
- The OD intervenor is an advocate for different values and behaviors than exist in most organizations at most times, and there is only danger in neglecting that the intervenor is consequently "in politics." The apparently simple act of affecting the quality and quantity of communication is an inherently political act, for example, and can be profoundly political in the sense of influencing who gets what, when, and why.
- In a continuing way, then, the OD intervenor is (and should be) a point man for a set of specific values and attendant behaviors, along with implications for appropriate organizational structures and practices. In military parlance, a "point man" is a key person on patrols: the point man is not in command, but does play a central role and can become the focus of enemy fire.
- The OD intervenor must be especially active and attentive to the "depth" of interventions, pitching interventions at the level appropriate to the presenting issues, to the apparent intentions of the host, and to the probability that learning goals can be attained without creating other and even less tractable issues than those addressed.

    In many cases, the conservative intervention will be one affecting structure or policies and procedures, rather than interaction. Here the OD intervenor must remain staunch, and resist the temptation to respect that traditional wisdom that all OD interventions involve *ab initio* a long-run program of cultural change.
- In many cases, interaction-centered approaches will require quick reinforcement by changes in structures, lest frustration and even despair result. So the intervenor must be aggressive in assessing the probability that such reinforcing changes will follow. Absent a substantial confidence, "No" often will be an appropriate intervention.

So what is there in the Superman metaphor-cum-message that got to so many people, so quickly and intensely? Opinions will differ, of course, but I have over time developed a substantially stable view. Basically, the Superman metaphor-cum-message threatens certain convenient *and* generally useful features of the common wisdom with regard to OD interventions. Five such threatened features illustrate the present case.

First, the reference to Superman may have been associated in some people's minds with the charismatic stimulators who had markedly higher casualty rates in training groups.[1]

The Wonder Woman/Superman metaphor could reasonably lead to such concerns, but the associated message should tether those concerns. Basically, the role elements suggest an active intervenor, but with the activity being personal gatekeeping and modeling. This contrasts sharply with precipitating others into what might become uncomfortable situations. In fact, the prescriptions here call for the opposite—that is, using the intervenor's role and person to reduce the probability that others are put in uncomfortable or even dangerous situations.

Second, the metaphor-and-message run counter to most prevailing verbalisms associated with OD interventions, and especially with their T-Group-oriented predecessors. Thus the truth-love model contrasts quite sharply with the point-man image; and the staunchness about "No" stands in opposition to sharing, involvement and participation.

Third, much of the conceptualization about intervention suggests a facilitator-only role, and the views abstracted above add substantial content to that role. The facilitator role serves to maximally reinforce many other features usefully associated with OD: the emphasis on choice by the client, on the client's ownership and commitment, and so on. This is all well and good, but only up to some more or less clearly designated points, which may be generally circumscribed by the intervenor's special skills and knowledge—in design, in what has worked in similar settings, and in access to the behavioral and organizational literature.

Fourth, the facilitator role places responsibility squarely with the client. In general, this is precisely where it should be. In extreme forms, however, the insistence borders on denying any conceptual basis for the OD intervenor, which may be accurate in cases but hardly amounts to the ideal situation in depicting the skilled and knowledgeable resource person.

Fifth, the facilitator-only role implies minimal skills and especially conceptual competencies. The present metaphor-and-message implies more open-ended demands.

As noted, these and other conventional denotations associated with intervening are convenient and even generally useful, but "generally useful" needs to be underscored. To be sure, there is danger in extensions from any historic baseline; but opportunities also become available when extensions are attempted.

In sum, the Superman metaphor-with-message intends some extensions from a historic baseline, and this accounts for its energizing qualities for both proponents and opponents of the extensions. For the debators recognized in a specific case what the Chinese language recognized for a long time. That is, I am told, the Chinese pictogram for ''change'' is composed of pictograms for two other words: ''danger'' and ''opportunity.'' And so it seems to be in this case, which sees an emerging balance as defining the role of OD intervenor. In global terms, the intervenor is an on-call facilitator, but with some energizable tendencies toward Wonder Woman and Superman.

Note

1. Morton A. Lieberman, Irvin D. Yalom, and Matthew B. Miles, *Encounter Groups* (New York: Basic Books, 1973).

34

ODers as Servants of Power: Temptations and Countertendencies

Perhaps the stock criticism of OD activities sees them as a con, with ODers serving as mere shills for management or other establishments. Two approaches to this stock criticism will be sketched. Some attention will be given to the real temptations facing ODers to become servants of those in power. But the dominant emphasis will be on how to mobilize countertendencies to these temptations.

The simple and sovereign form of stock criticism has a directness that appeals to many. Typically, goes this argument, money talks. Management (or some other elite) determines OD missions and roles and also pays the bills for OD services. Hence, it is said to follow, ODers cannot help but be servants of those in power. Some ODers might struggle against such a tether, this position also proposes, but it is all futile in the end. The essence of this view is direct: the dollar dominates, sooner or later—and usually sooner.

Sophisticated forms of the stock criticism present more formidable problems, as in the case of labeling OD as a "mature or maturing industry." Briefly, this position distinguishes two periods in OD's history. "Then" was an idyllic time—of a small cadre of conscientious and devoted people working toward practical realization of humanistic ideals, committed to push forward the boundaries of an expanding *science plus art*. As in many frontier settings, *the* goal was paramount. Excitement—of past breakthroughs, as well as of those numerous future breakthroughs perceived to be just around the next corner—carried people over the inevitable rough spots. The spirit was upbeat and ebullient, with much evidence of cooperation and collaboration in pushing toward changes in ways of thinking and doing.

"Now" in this view of OD as mature or maturing industry has a very different profile. The small cadres of devotees have been overwhelmed by the legions. A minority of them remain idealists with practical skills and ambitions; but the vast majority are drawn by the opportunities for personal gain at what had been a frontier, but now grows increasingly crowded. Indeed, some are more anxious to score than they are committed to an ideal. They practice OD by razor blade, as it were. You know, their glass doors only recently carried such legends as "general management consultants," but they have been hurriedly replaced by such identifiers as "Organization Development Specialists," "Team-Building Facilitators," or some such. These replacements came mercurially—changes in outer signs that in many cases reflect little or no change in inner spirit, as it were.

The "now" view also reflects the impact of three massive factors on a suddenly overpopulated OD landscape. First, the demand for OD services dropped in the late 1970s, just as the supply had reached new peaks. Second, the perception grew that there was nothing new under the OD sun, in massive contrast to the limitless frontiers envisioned only a decade or so before. Third, the entry costs for "getting into OD" were escalating—some called for certification and peer review, graduate degrees in OD or related specialties become more common, and (perhaps especially) research had significantly raised the ante on the level of knowledge and skills that could pass even moderate tests of caring and competent practice.

In sum, this "now" view severely tempts ODers to become servants of those in power. Assignments should be more difficult to find, in this view of the OD world. And absent substantial and sudden out-migrations of ODers, the mature or maturing marketplace would encourage an unpleasant family of adaptions. These include:

- spurious differentiation of product lines
- competition via price reductions, with less concern for quality
- living off the past rather than contributing to the future, as by reductions in research and development
- being oversolicitous of the needs of powerful clients when cross-pressure situations arise, as they often will
- practical pressures grow and ethical sensitivity diminishes

There is a danger in sketching these two views of the ODer as shil, of course. Directly, some people might come to believe that they represent views of what dominates in the world, *of what is*. Worse still, some folks might take an either further leap: that the two views represent *what should be*.

Those are serious risks, and not lightly contemplated. But they have to be taken. The present view is dual: writing about these two variants of ODers as servants of power is no good thing; but *not* writing about them is far worse.

So let the present point be put boldly. Temptations do exist to fall into two kinds of adaptive error that can be labeled: the dollar dominates; and OD is a mature or maturing industry. No doubt, one can find examples of both classes of adaptive errors.

But note that one can respond to even strong temptations in very different ways. The critics typically assume the worse—that what I call "adaptive errors" will result. Although ODers can get bent out of shape ethically, the bulk of this volume is oriented toward energizing countertendencies to the kinds of temptations alluded to above.

On the premise that some things are so important that they bear even frequent repetition, lest they be forgotten, let me illustrate some of the countertendencies inherent in the essays in this book. Put directly, most (or even all) of the preceding essays can be viewed as building or energizing countertendencies to the kinds of temptations that ODers face. Although only illustration is possible here, it may be useful to sketch how several of the preceding selections serve the purpose just advertised. Five cases in point will serve to illustrate the broader catalog that might be developed.

1. Personal and professional values are major bulwarks against temptation, whether in gross forms or subtle. Hence several of the preceding essays direct attention to values and norms. This emphasis comes early in this volume, as in "Why OD?: Putting Values in Their Prominent Place." Careful readers also will detect the trail of this theme in the book's middle ranges, as in "Not Whether to Market, but What." And the emphasis appears very late, as in the essay " 'Promise Not to Tell': A Critical View of Confidentiality in Consultation."

2. A flinty resolve to trust and to test one's technology will be a bulwark against becoming a mere servant of power. Several selections urge both trusting and testing, which at first blush may seem an unlikely duo but are inextricably linked, as even a little reflection should establish. "Process Observation as *the* Key: Where and When to Practice Skills?" provides one variation on this theme. Moreover, the several selections dealing with the assessment of OD effects patently focus on trust/test: for example, "So What About Success Rates?"; and "An Even Better Kept Secret: Success Rates in Third-World Applications."

3. An action-orientation to extend OD technology and values, broadly and deeply, provides a useful defense against the two kinds of temptation sketched above. This may involve serving low-power as well as high-power clients, which is part of the burden of "We Are Not Here to Reinvent the *Status Quo*." Or the orientation may be reflected in an ODer's caution as to who becomes a client. In this connection, see the pair of essays titled "Judas Goats and Providing or Withholding Consultation" and "Value Complementarity and Providing or Withholding Consultation."

4. Peer review and accreditation can be powerful stimuli for highlighting the sense of ethical practice. The interested reader might review two essays in this regard: "Professionalization, Performance, and Protectionism": A Contingency View; and " 'It's Not My Dog, Mister' : The Issue of OD Certification."

5. Various institutional devices can reinforce and sustain the sense of competent and caring practice. The essays above include broad and narrow perspectives on this critical point. "Toward a National Institute of Planned and Peaceful Change: Visioning About Our Future" presents a broad view; and "The Fund for Displaced ODers" provides narrower perspective on how institutional devices can provide countertendencies to the temptations ODers face.

Name Index

Subject Index

Action research, ix, 46, 73–74; in Bombay, 46; and participatory research, 46; and river blindness, 73–74; and "straight science," ix, 73–74; and survey feedback, 46
Agreement, crisis of, as contrasted with crisis of disagreement, 67–68
Agriculture, U.S. Department of, 134
American Productivity Managers' Association, 106
American Society for Training and Development, 152
Army, U.S., 13, 119–20; and training in OD, 13

"Bethel" experience, 36

Center for the Study of Ethics in the Professions, Illinois Institute of Technology, 130, 144
Certification in OD, 120–30; a contingency view of, 121–26; factors encouraging performance, 122–23; factors encouraging protectionism, 123–25; the ideal, 120–21; some institutions affecting progress toward, 120–23; a shaggy-dog story about, 127–28; a Statement of Values and Ethics for, 129–30
Certified Consultants International, or CCI, 37–38, 129, 144
Confidentiality, 165–72; restricted, 167–68; some guides for action, 171–72; and trust, 166–72; two cases of, 168–71; unrestricted, 166–67
Consultation in OD, 52–90, 109–16, 129–30, 143–54, 178–79; in business vs. public sectors, 59–70; some differences in public sector, 66–69; and ethical issues, 52–56, 129–30; generic features of, 58–66; and Judas Goats, 109–11; awkward modes of, 111–12; a Statement of Values and Ethics for,

129–30, 143–46, 156; value complementarity in, 109–16; and withholding of services, 109–16
Cooling-out roles, 119
Corning Glass, 119
Culture, in OD, 7–8, 64–66, 85–103, 157–59; and boundedness by, 7–8, 64–66; features of, 65–66, 88–90, 157–59; and success rates, 79–80, 85–103
Culture-boundedness in OD, 58–66, 71–75; the case for, 71–72; the case against, 58–66, 73–76

Degenerative interaction, 20–21, 166–72; as anti-goal in OD, 20–21; consequences of, 21; and openness, 20–21; and owning, 20–21; and risk, 20–21; and trust, 20–21, 166–72
Demotion experience, 116
Diagnosis, 58–70; as central in OD, 58–70; and crisis of agreement vs. crisis of conflict, 67–68
Diffusion in OD, 20–21, 82, 113–14, 116–72; by "seeding," 82, 113–14; and "critical mass," 82, 113–14; and regenerative interaction, 20–21, 82, 166–72

Esso, early OD in, 43

Flexible workhours, 115
Flexner report, 122
Freedom, responsible, in organizations, 23–26

Generations in OD, 30–41; basic orientations of, 31–34; four generational rosters, 30–31; and supporting institutions, 37–38; training and background of, 36–37; and values vs. technologies, 33, 38–40
"Groupthink," 67

Institute of, 131–34; features of, 132–34; in OD's future, 131–32

Politics/administration interface, 58

Populism and elitism, 38–39, 42–47; in Indian intervention, 46; in OD, 42–47; and orientations to change, 44–46

Power/coercion in OD, 49

Process observation, 4–5, 12–14, 20–21, 31–33; and "expert model," 12; features of, 12–14; and OD, 4–5, 12–14; in OD generations, 31–33; practice for, 13; and regenerative interaction, 20–21

"Process" vs. "product," emphasis on, 28, 31–33

Quality circles, 9

Quality of Working Life, or QWL, 31, 91, 104–8; and contrasts with OD, 104–6; and OD's preeminence, 106–7; and flexibility of values, 106–7

Regenerative interaction, 20–21, 166–72; centrality of in OD, 20–21; consequences of, 21; and openness, 20–21; and owning, 20–21; and risk, 20–21; and trust, 20–21, 166–72

Risk, 20–21; centrality of in OD, 20–21; features of, 20

Role negotiation, 16

SmithKline Corp., 119

Society for Participatory Research, 47

Strategic planning, 120

Success of OD applications, 85–103; in economically-disadvantaged settings, 91–94; high rates of in western settings, 85–87; reasons for lack of emphasis on, 95–103; substantial rates of in third-world settings, 88–90

"Support groups," 12

Team-building, 24, 109–11, 161–62; ethical issues in, 109–11

Technostructural approaches, 105

Tennessee Valley Authority, 63

T-Groups, 12–13, 16, 33; in OD, 12–13, 16

Trust, 20–21, 166–72; centrality of in OD, 20–21; and confidentiality, 166–72; features of, 20

Unions and OD, 105

University Associates, 13, 117

Value complementarity in providing or withholding consultation, 113–16; and comprehensive social change, 114–15; and limited-purpose contracts, 115–16

Values, 5–8, 18–26, 52–75, 106–16, 129–30, 143–46, 156–60; complementarity of, 109–11, 113–16; and consultation, 52–70, 109–16; and culture, 7–8, 64–66, 71–75; 157–60; and ethical issues in OD practice, 52–56, 129–30, 143–46, 156; and "needs models," 18–19; in OD, 5–8, 18–22; and OD generations, 33; and QWL, 106–7; and regenerative interaction, 20–21, 25–26; and responsible freedom in organization, 23–26; and a Statement for Values and Ethics, 129–30, 143–46, 156

Visioning in OD, 82–83, 131–34

"Zeigarnik effect," 151